# 4

*Ingredients*

# 2

**4 Ingredients**
**PO box 1171**
**Mooloolaba QLD 4557**

ABN:    19 307 118 068

www.4ingredients.com.au
info@4ingredients.com.au

Design:      Nigel Forbes
Typesetting:   BlueCrystal Creative; www.bluecrystalcreative.com
Cartoon image of Rachael & Kim by: Faster pussycat productions www.fppdesign.com.au
Printed & bound in Australia by McPherson's Printing Group, Maryborough Victoria

AUS Distributor: Gary Allen (02) 9725 2440
NZ Distributor:   Random House

**ISBN: 978-0 -646-49179-0**

# Foreword

WELL ... WHO WOULD EVER HAVE THOUGHT ... Two girls who met 37 years ago would not only remain friends into adulthood, but also join forces to write the biggest selling Cookbook not only in Australia but also New Zealand for 2007!!! Even more amazingly go on to write this, our second 4 Ingredients cookbook!

Every day, we are asked just how we did it. A few things you may know: it was Kim who had the idea for this concept and kept it under her hat for a few years before approaching Rachael, who had previously written and self published a book and who had the marketing know how. Together we pooled our talents to construct a cookbook we needed in our everyday lives ... *THAT WAS THE EASY PART!!!*

But what most people don't know is that no publisher shared our enthusiasm and vision for what a godsend this book actually was – *THIS WAS THE HARD PART!!!* We tag teamed and called every publisher in Australia we could get a phone number for, and even one in New Zealand! Whilst we thought we had a winner, they thought otherwise with responses ranging from ' Are you famous?', 'Oh not another cookbook' to the classic one ' CLUNK!'

Fortunately we are resilient, so we simply sought other avenues to make it happen. Kim stepped up to the plate and funded the setup and printing of the book while Rachael got busy setting up a website and marketing plan that would ensure that the book would sell. In the meantime, however, we still had one major challenge, and that was we didn't have any distribution channel other than OURSELVES!!!!

We called 4 distributors and all refused but one! We had the great fortune to be connected to the operations manager, Ed Petrie of Sydney based distributor Gary Allen. To his absolute credit, he listened to us and didn't hang up!!! In fact by the end of the conversation he asked us to send him a copy!!!!!!!!!!!!!! Even *MORE* to his credit, he accepted our draft copy as we hadn't yet printed the book!

Three long weeks of waiting were finally over when Ed called back saying that of the 10 self-published titles they see across their desks every week, of the less than one title a month they accept ... Ours was one of them. *YAAAAAYYYYYYYY!!!!!!* What we didn't realise of course was that this meant all 1,000 books we sent to them were strictly on consignment basis and that we would have to wait for them to be ordered by booksellers, then wait three months before our first payday ... We had to create demand!

From there, each day when our 3 beautiful boys had a nap, we began to implement our marketing plan. We sent our press release to every radio station, newspaper, magazine and TV program in the country AND followed up each with a phone call. We also rang every bookstore in Australia, we introduced ourselves, told them about our terrific book and thanked them in advance for ANY support they could hand our way!

We organised book-signings from one end of this vast country to the other, we booked motels and hotels, flights, taxis and hire cars all at our expense. We did this all around our families daily lives and activities and knowing we had the love and support of our wonderful husbands Glen and Paul, because without them we would have been unable to travel.

We are often told that we don't realise just what we did in 2007... From our initial 2,000 we went on to print over 420,000 books for the year!!!!!!!!! And truth be told, we still don't think about the magnitude of it. All we did (and still do) is put in lots of time and work to achieve what we wanted to do in the only way we knew how ... hard work! We also had an enormous amount of good fortune along the way, such as being blessed with remarkable families and friends. We are extremely grateful to for their generosity; giving freely of their time, their love and support without which we could not have achieved all that we did!

To Ed Petrie, we single you out because you went in to bat for our book with a gut feeling it could work and for you, we are *soooooo* glad it did. You do what you do brilliantly and we thank you for taking a chance on us.

To the booksellers who embraced us and supported us, who kept ordering, telling people about it, and continue to do so ... We thank you very much.

To everyone who believed our story, and thought it good enough to print, to interview, to film for various audiences we thank you for helping us to spread the love ... You are sensational and we really appreciate it!

To all who sent (in particular the *very generous* Marie McColl) or emailed recipes through, thank you so much.  The ideas you had were just too good to keep to ourselves, and it is from you the inspiration for this second book sprang!

We hope sharing our story also inspires you to do whatever it is you are thinking of doing, because you never know where a good idea, a bit of motivation, and a tonne of work may lead you!!!!!

And finally, *THANK YOU* for being part of our journey by owning a copy of our book.

Best Wishes & Happy Cooking

# KIM & RACHAEL

Kim                Rachael

## www.4ingredients.com.au

*For more detailed information on how we wrote our books and how we made them the bestsellers they are, please visit our website www.4ingredients.com.au where you will find a mini-book we wrote about it.*

# In The Cupboard

In 4 Ingredients 2 we have a suggestion of ingredients you may want to stock to help you create many a wonderful meals and treats from the pages within! *Please note: Again, in this book we have not included salt, pepper & water as part of the 4 ingredients.*

| Savoury | Sweet |
|---|---|
| Basil Pesto | Arrowroot biscuits |
| BBQ Sauce | Caster sugar |
| Beef & chicken stock cubes | Cinnamon |
| Breadcrumbs | Condensed milk |
| Cold pressed macadamia nut oil | Cornflour |
| Curry powder | Cream |
| Dijon mustard | Cream cheese |
| Extra virgin macadamia oil spray | Desiccated coconut |
| French onion soup (dry mix) | Eggs |
| Fresh vegetables | Evaporated milk |
| Garlic | Food colouring |
| Lemons | Fresh fruit |
| Minced ginger | Gelatine |
| Peppercorns | Honey |
| Pine nuts | Icing sugar |
| Rice | Jams: Apricot, strawberry |
| Sea salt | Jelly crystals |
| Sesame seeds | Marmalade |
| Shortcrust Pastry | Mixed fruit (homebrand) |
| Spaghetti & noodles | Mixed spices |
| Sour cream | Nutmeg |
| Soy sauce | Plain & self raising flour |
| Sweet chilli sauce | Pkt. bamboo skewers |
| Tinned soups: Asparagus, Celery etc. | Pkt. vanilla cake mix |
| Tomato sauce | Puff pastry (preferably with butter) |
| Whole-egg mayonnaise | Sugar (raw, brown) |
| Worcestershire sauce | Tinned fruit: Pineapple, pear |
| Vegetable Seasoning | Tin of pie apple |
| Vegetable Stock | Vanilla essence |
| Vinegar | |

# Guide to weights and measures

A big fancy conversion table is not required, as all you need to make the recipes within 4 Ingredients are:

1 Teaspoon (tsp.)

1 Tablespoon (tbs.)

1 Cup

*... and a pinch of love!!*

# Abbreviations used

| | |
|---|---|
| Gram | g |
| Kilogram | kg |
| Millilitre | ml |
| Litre | ltr |

# Oven temperature guide

Making friends with your oven really helps when cooking. Basically the Celsius temperature is about half the Fahrenheit temperature.

A lot of ovens these days offer the option to bake or fan bake (amongst others); as a rule, the fan-assisted option will greatly increase the temperature in your oven and will shorten cooking times.

Our recipes have been compiled assuming a fan-forced oven, unless otherwise stated. If however your oven is conventional, as a general rule of thumb, fan-forced cooking temperatures are increased by 20C (this may vary between models). So if the recipe reads bake for 1 hour at 200C that will be 1 hour at 220 conventional.

**Here's some help:**

| | Fahrenheit | Celsius | Gas Mark |
|---|---|---|---|
| Slow | 275 | 140 | 1 |
| Slow | 300 | 150 | 2 |
| Mod | 325 | 165 | 3 |
| Mod | 350 | 180 | 4 |
| Mod hot | 375 | 190 | 5 |
| Mod hot | 400 | 200 | 6 |
| Hot | 425 | 220 | 7 |
| Hot | 450 | 230 | 8 |
| Very hot | 475 | 240 | 9 |

# Healthy Food Substitutes

What we would really have loved is to have substituted many of our everyday household products for healthier alternatives. The main reason being is that natural, non-technically enhanced products are LOADED with essential nutrients that fuel your body, mind and soul. Apart form the obvious short and long term benefits of consuming these ingredients, you can literally taste the difference.

However not wanting to isolate those that are not able to purchase these products readily, we did not include these within our recipes, opting instead to add this section, which we feel, is vital to your and your families' health. For those of you able to access these products readily the table below will show you what mainstream ingredient can be easily substituted with a healthier (and less technically altered and therefore nutrient drained) alternative. For more information on this we recommend our good friend Cyndi O'Meara's book Changing Habits Changing Lives:

| Product | Substitute |
|---------|-----------|
| Sugar | • Brown Sugar / Organic Raw Sugar* |
| Oil | • Cold pressed Extra Virgin Olive Oil* |
| | • Cold Pressed Macadamia Nut Oil* |
| Spray Oil | • Cold Pressed Macadamia Nut Oil * |
| Flour | • Spelt Flour |
| | • Organic Plain Flour |
| | • Organic Self Raising Flour |
| Margarine | • Butter |
| Eggs | • Free Range Eggs* |
| Milk | • Organic Milk* |
| | • Raw Milk (pasteurised only milk) |
| Pasta | • Made from fresh ingredients |
| | • Organic Pasta* |
| Honey | • Manuka Honey* |
| | • Organic Honey* |
| Jams | • Organic Jam* |
| | • Homemade Jams made from raw ingredients |
| Soy Sauce | • Tamari Soy Sauce* |

*Note – all ingredients with an asterisk * can now be bought in your local supermarket.*

# Table of Contents

# Breakfasts

"The strength of a civilization should not be measured by its ability to win wars, but by its ability to prevent them."

**Gene Roddenberry**

---

## A Campfire Egg

**Makes 4**

- *4 eggs*
- *2 oranges*

Cut oranges in half and eat the pulp.  Crack an egg into the orange skin and place it in the embers until the egg turns white.

## Basic Crepes

**Makes 30**

- *3 eggs*
- *1½ cups milk*
- *2¼ cups plain flour*
- *1 tsp. macadamia nut oil*

Blend all ingredients together with 1½ cups of water. Heat a non-stick frying pan and add the oil swirling around to coat the entire surface.  Pour about ¼ cup of mixture into the pan and swirl in a circular motion outwards so the batter is even.  Cook for about 2 minutes or until the bottom is light brown and flip over to cook other side, repeat until mixture is gone.

# Breakfast Dish

**Serves 4**

- *4 slices bread*
- *1 carrot, grated*
- *1 cup grated cheese*
- *6 eggs, beaten*

Preheat oven to 180C. Place bread in a square dish and cover with carrot and beaten eggs, season with sea salt and pepper. Sprinkle cheese on top and bake until the eggs are set and the cheese is melted and bubbling.

*Optional: Substitute carrot for whatever vegetable you like.*

# Baked Raspberry French Toast

**Serves 6. A deliciously different way to prepare French toast.**

- *¾ cup raspberry jam*
- *12 slices wholemeal bread, remove crusts*
- *6 eggs*
- *1 cup milk*

Spread jam on 1 side of 6 slices of bread and cover with remaining bread to form 6 sandwiches. Beat eggs and milk until frothy. Pour just enough egg mixture into well greased pan to cover bottom of a baking dish. Arrange sandwiches in pan. Pour remaining egg mixture over top. Bake in 230C oven for about 20 minutes until golden and egg is set.

# Blueberry Pancakes

**Makes 6**

- *1 cup self raising flour*
- *1 cup soya milk*
- *1 egg*
- *½ cup fresh blueberries*

Combine first 3 ingredients in a bowl, add blueberries and mix well. Cook in ¼ cup portions in a non-stick frying pan over medium-low heat.  Wait for bubbles to appear before flipping.

*Optional:  Fabulous served with citrus-infused maple syrup.  To make; simply take half a cup of maple syrup and to it add a large piece of orange peel, allow to sit for flavours to infuse.*


# Cafe Style Scrambled Eggs

**Serves 2.  Recipe from Kelly Mauger.**

- *4 eggs*
- *½ cup pouring cream*

In a microwave-safe dish, beat ingredients and season.
Cook for 2½ minutes on high or until it starts to rise.
Remove and serve on toast.

# Caramel Bananas

**Makes 4.  A recipe by the adorable Brett McCosker.**

- *4 bananas*
- *¾ cup brown sugar*
- *3 tbs. butter*
- *4 pancakes*


Cook bananas in butter and sugar over low heat in a fry pan until bananas are soft and caramelised.  Place each pancake on a plate and pour over the mixture.


# Caramelised Croissants

**Serves 4**

- *4 croissants*
- *1 tbs. butter*
- *2 large bananas*
- *2 tbs. brown sugar*


Preheat grill to 180C.  Halve each croissant and spread with butter. Top equally with sliced banana and then sprinkle with brown sugar. Grill until golden brown and serve warm.

# Creamy Choc-Strawberry Waffles

**Serves 6**

- *8 warm waffles*
- *¼ cup Nutella or Hazelnut spread*
- *¾ cup fresh ricotta*
- *8 big, ripe strawberries, washed, hulled and chopped*

Toast waffles.  Combine nutella and ricotta.  Spread evenly over waffles and top with strawberries.


# Grilled Fruit with Muesli Yoghurt

**Serves 4**

- *8 ripe nectarines*
- *2-3 tbs. honey*
- *1 tsp. ground cinnamon*
- *400g tubs of Greek style yoghurt with toasted muesli*

Preheat grill on high.  Line a baking tray with alfoil.  Place fruit cut side up, drizzle with honey to lightly coat and sprinkle evenly with cinnamon.  Grill until syrup bubbles and fruit begins to char.  Serve warm with dollops of yoghurt and muesli mix.

*Optional:  Substitute nectarines for pears, peaches or whatever fruit is in season.  Nearly any Greek yoghurt combination works with this.*

# French Toast

**Serves 4.  Recipe by the charming Cyndi O'Meara.**

- *4 pieces of stale bread*
- *4 eggs*
- *½ cup milk*
- *¼ tsp. mixed spice*

Beat eggs and milk and spice together, soak bread in the mixture, once bread is soaked place into hot non-stick pan and cook on both sides until just golden in colour.

*Optional:  Serve with fresh fruit and real maple syrup.*

# Lemon Butter

**A sensational spread for breakfast from the beautiful Dymphna Boholt.**

- *½ cup butter*
- *1½ cups sugar*
- *3 eggs*
- *3 lemons*

Melt butter, add sugar and well-beaten eggs and the juice of the lemons.  Cook over gentle heat until thick.  Pour into jar and store in fridge.

*Optional:  Grate in the zest of a lemon.  For  passionfruit butter, omit zest and use ½ cup passionfruit pulp and ¼ cup lemon juice.*

*Hint:  In the microwave:  Melt butter and sugar.  In a separate bowl, beat eggs with a beater until frothy.  Juice the lemons and add them and the eggs to the butter mix.  Cook on med/high for 5 minutes stirring every minute.*

# Morning Mushies

**Serves 2.  A recipe from Jan Neale.**

- *1 tsp. butter*
- *1 cup button mushrooms, sliced*
- *½ cup cream*
- *2 slices thick wholemeal bread*

Heat butter in frying pan over moderate heat.  Cook mushrooms, stirring, for 3-5 minutes.  Add cream, gently stir until sauce thickens.  Season to taste with black pepper.  Serve over toast.

*Optional:  Sprinkle with freshly chopped chives.*

*Hint:  Don't peel mushrooms before cooking as most of the flavour and nutritional value is just below the skin.*

# Muesli Smoothie

**Serves 1-2.  A recipe from the lovely Kim Morrison.**

- *1 cup milk or soy milk*
- *1 frozen banana*
- *½ cup toasted muesli*
- *3 tbs. fruit yoghurt*

Place all ingredients in blender and process until smooth.

*Optional:  Add ice if you would like it colder.*

# Orange & Prune Crunch Cereal

**Serves 2**

- *200g tub flavoured yoghurt*
- *1 medium orange, peeled*
- *5 medium prunes, stones removed*
- *½ cup oats*

Place the yoghurt in a medium bowl.  Slice the orange flesh thinly and stir into the yoghurt with the prunes and rolled oats.


# Quick Bircher Muesli

**Serves 1.  Recipe by Cyndi O'Meara.**

- *¼ cup oats*
- *1 banana*
- *½ cup strawberry yoghurt*
- *1 tbs. chopped nuts*

Soak oats in water overnight.  In the morning, drain, chop banana, add nuts and yoghurt and combine, served chilled.

*Optional:  Add whatever fruit you like.*

# Quick Muffins

**Makes 6**

- *1 cup self raising flour*
- *4 tbs. whole egg mayonnaise*
- *¾ cup milk*
- *4 rashes of bacon, diced and fried*

Mix all ingredients until just combined. Fill muffin cups two-thirds full. Bake in a preheated oven at 180C for about 15-20 minutes.

*Optional: Substitute bacon for whatever you like.*

# Spinach Dampers

**Makes 6**

- *250g pkt frozen spinach, chopped and thawed*
- *2 cups self raising flour*
- *200ml sour cream*

Preheat oven 220C. Line a baking tray with paper. Squeeze excess liquid from spinach. Place flour in a bowl and add sour cream, stir to combine. Add spinach and mix by hand to make a sticky dough. Turn out onto a floured surface and kneed until smooth. Shape into 6 balls and place on tray. Bake for 15 minutes.

*Optional: Grated zucchini, or a can of corn can be used instead of spinach. Top with grated parmesan cheese prior to baking.*

# Sweet Breakfast Toast

**Makes 1.  Recipe by Cyndi O'Meara.**

- *1 slice bread*
- *1 tsp. peanut butter*
- *1 tsp. honey*
- *1 small banana, mashed*

Toast the bread, first spread with peanut butter, then honey, then banana.

*Optional:  Sprinkle with pine nuts.*

# Tomato Jam

- *3kg ripe tomatoes*
- *2kg sugar*
- *4 lemons*

Skin tomatoes by scalding for a few minutes in boiling water, place in a large saucepan with sugar, lemon juice and finely shredded rind. Boil rapidly until jam sets when tested.  Bottle.

*Hint:  If making jam be sure that your jars are heated to seal well.  Rest them in hot water and dry quickly before filling each jar.*

# Dips, Salad Dressings & Sauces

*"If we could give every individual
the right amount of nourishment and exercise,
not too little and not too much, we would have found
the safest way to health."*

**Hippocrates**

---

## Bailey's Dip Delight

**Serves 10. This is a favourite for all gatherings by the gorgeous Jules Boag.**

- *¼ cup Baileys liqueur*
- *¼ cup brown sugar*
- *1½ cups sour cream*

Mix all ingredients together and serve with fresh strawberries or slice a fresh pineapple, cutting out the core in one slice and putting a heaped dollop in the centre of the pineapple. Use the rest of the pineapple as dipping chips.

## Basil Dip

**Makes 1 cup. Recipe by Laurent Vancam.**

- *1 bunch of fresh basil*
- *2 tsp. minced garlic*
- *¾ cup grated parmesan cheese*
- *¼ cup of extra virgin olive oil*

Blend all ingredients together and serve. Easy and ultra tasty!

---

# Chutney & Cheese Dip

**Makes approx. 1 cup**

- *125g cream cheese*
- *3 tbs. of mixed fruit chutney*
- *¼ tsp. curry powder*
- *Freshly cracked pepper*

Mix all ingredients together, chill before serving with your favourite crackers or vege sticks.


# Cinnamon Dip

**Makes 1 cup.  A *sensational* recipe by Shane McCosker.**

- *250g sour cream*
- *1 generous tsp. ground cinnamon*
- *1 tbs. brown sugar*

Place all ingredients into a bowl and mix well.  Chill for at least 2 hours prior to serving to allow flavours time to develop.  Serve with a platter of fresh fruit and dried apricots for dipping.


# Corn Chips

**Makes 32**

- *4 corn tortillas, cut into 8 pieces*
- *½ cup olive oil*

Place oil in a large saucepan and heat until hot.  Cook corn tortillas in batches for 1-2 minutes or until crisp and golden.  Drain on soaking paper and sprinkle with sea salt.

# Date Dip

**Makes 1 cup. Rich and delicious.**

- *250g pkt dates*
- *½ cup sour cream*

Chop dates finely. Bring dates and ½ cup water to boil and simmer for a few minutes until most of the water is absorbed. Cool date mixture then blend thoroughly with cream. Chill for several hours before serving with a mezze of fresh fruit.


# Easy Creamy Dip

**Makes 1 cup. A recipe by the dynamic Deb Wheeler.**

- *½ cup Praise mayonnaise*
- *½ cup sour cream*
- *1-2 garlic cloves, crushed*

Mix all ingredients together and serve chilled with fresh broccoli and cauliflower florets.

# Feta Dip

**Makes 1 cup and is *really, really* tasty.**

- *200g feta*
- *¼ cup olive oil*
- *2 garlic cloves, crushed*
- *¼ cup milk*

Place feta, oil and 1 clove of crushed garlic into a food processor and blend until combined. Whilst still processing, gently add milk in a slow stream and mix until a smooth paste forms. Chill before serving.

*Optional: Serve with melba toast or fresh vege sticks.*

# Home Style Corn Chips

**Serves 4.  A healthier option for your dips by Maz Lacy.**

- *4 slices pita bread*
- *Macadamia nut oil spray*
- *3 tbs. lemon pepper or garlic salt*

Preheat oven to 160C.  Cut pita bread into corn chip size pieces and spray with macadamia nut oil (or olive oil).  Sprinkle with lemon pepper and bake for 6-10 minutes or until crispy.


# Melba Toast

**Makes 16**

- *4 slices of wholemeal bread*

Remove crusts and cut each piece of bread diagonally into quarters.  Place on a baking tray and bake in 180C oven for 6 minutes or until lightly golden and crisp.

*Optional:  You can roll bread thinner if preferred.*


# Nutty Blue Cheese Dip

**Makes 1 cup**

- *250g cream cheese*
- *3½ tbs. whole egg mayonnaise*
- *½ cup crumbled blue cheese*
- *4 tbs. chopped walnuts, toasted*

Beat cream cheese and mayonnaise in a bowl until smooth.  Add cheese and walnuts.  Chill and serve with a mezze of fresh vege sticks or crackers.

# Parmesan, Caper & Basil Spread

**Makes 1¼ cup.  A recipe from Janelle McCosker.**

- *250g cream cheese, softened*
- *½ cup finely grated parmesan*
- *1½ tbs. capers, rinsed and roughly chopped*
- *1½ tbs. finely chopped fresh basil*

Blend cheeses in a bowl.  Add capers and basil, season with pepper.  Refrigerate for at least 1 hour before serving.  This allows time for the flavours to develop.

# Red Yoghurt Dip

- *¼ cup drained capsicum*
- *1 cup Greek yoghurt*

Puree capsicum with yoghurt.  Chill and serve with crusty French bread or a mezze of vege sticks.

# Tapenade

**Makes approx. 1 cup**

- *2/3 cup kalamata olives*
- *1 clove garlic, crushed*
- *2 tbs. finely chopped, fresh basil*
- *1½ tbs. olive oil*

Place ingredients in a blender and process until smooth.  Cover, chill and when needed serve with crackers.

# Salmon Savoury Log

**Serves 6-8**

- *415g can pink salmon*
- *2 spring onions, finely chopped*
- *125g feta cheese*
- *½ cup chopped parsley*

Drain salmon and remove bones. Crumble feta cheese and combine with salmon, add spring onions. Shape into a log and roll in parsley. Chill and serve with slices of cucumber or melba toast.

*Hint: Parsley is the world's most popular herb. It contains three times as much vitamin C as oranges, twice as much iron as spinach, is rich in vitamin A and contains folate, potassium and calcium.*

# Toblerone Dip

**Makes 1 cup. A recipe from the lovely Donna McCosker that will have your guests asking for more!**

- *100g Toblerone*
- *2 tbs. whipping cream*
- *1 tbs. honey*

In microwave jug, melt Toblerone on low heat for 2 minutes, stirring every 15 seconds. Mix through cream and honey and serve with a mezze of fresh fruit to dip.

*Hint: When recipe calls for spoonfuls of honey or golden syrup use a spoon that's been dipped in hot water. The mixture will slip off the spoon more easily.*

# Warm Cheese Dip

**Makes 2 cups.  This is *R.e.a.l.l.y Y.u.m.m.y!!!***

- *2 tbs. butter*
- *¾ cup sour cream*
- *2 cups grated cheddar cheese*
- *½ tsp. ground cumin*

Melt butter in saucepan and add cumin, stir over a low heat for a minute.  Add sour cream and when warm, add cheddar cheese.  Stir constantly until the cheese melts and the mixture is smooth.  Serve warm with crackers or fresh crusty bread.

# Salad Dressings

The most important thing in life is to know when to seize opportunities and when to abandon interests.

**Someone wise!**

---

## Apricot and Tahini Dressing

**Makes ¾ cup.  Recipe by Gabrielle Bluett.**

- *2 tbs. apricot jam*
- *½ cup tahini*
- *1 tsp. mustard*
- *1-2 tbs. rice vinegar*

Mix all ingredients together.

## Balsamic Dressing

**Makes 1 cup.  Recipe by Tracey Stevens who describes it as "A yummy, creamy dressing."**

- *100mls (slightly less than ½ cup) vegetable oil (do not use olive oil)*
- *2 tsp. Dijon mustard*
- *1/3 cup milk*
- *2 tbs. balsamic vinegar*

Mix the oil, mustard and milk together in a screw top jar and shake to combine.  Add the balsamic vinegar and shake again.

# Blue Cheese Dressing

**Makes 1 cup**

- *30g blue cheese*
- *1/3 cup whole egg mayonnaise*
- *1/3 cup natural yoghurt*
- *3 tbs. freshly chopped chives*

Mash cheese in a small bowl using a fork. Add remaining ingredients and mix well. Season to taste with black pepper.


# Buttermilk Dressing

**Makes ½ cup. Recipe by Gabrielle Bluett.**

- *1/3 cup buttermilk*
- *1 tbs. balsamic vinegar*
- *1 tbs. lemon juice*
- *½ tsp mustard*

Mix all ingredients thoroughly.


# Classic Salad Dressing

**Makes 1 cup and forever stands the test of time!**

- *¼ cup fresh lemon juice*
- *2 tbs. olive extra virgin olive oil*
- *1 tsp. Dijon mustard*
- *1 clove garlic, crushed*

Place all in a screw top jar, season to taste and shake well.

*Hint: When a jar of mustard is nearly empty, add some olive oil and wine vinegar and shake well for a delicious salad dressing.*

# Caramelised Balsamic Vinegar

**Makes ¼ cup**

- 2/3 cup balsamic vinegar
- ½ cup brown sugar

Bring ingredients to the boil slowley.  Stir until dissolve sugar. Boil for 1 minute or untill slightly thick.  Allow to cool and store in refrigerator.

# Easy Salad Dressing

- 2 tbs. lemon juice
- ¼ cup olive oil

Mix well lemon juice and oil and season with sea salt and pepper.

# Feta Dressing

- 100g feta cheese, crumbled finely
- 1 clove garlic, crushed
- ½ cup French salad dressing

Place all ingredients in a jar and shake vigorously.

# Flavoured Oils

## Chilli

- 20 seeded and chopped chillies
- 1 cup macadamia nut oil

*Place chillies into a heatproof container. Heat oil in a small frying pan until it just reaches smoking point, leave to cool for 10 minutes then pour over the chillies and leave for at least 1½ hours. Strain into a clean bottle and keep in refrigerator.*

## Garlic

- 1 garlic clove, peel and halved
- 2 cups extra virgin olive oil

Peel and halve a large garlic clove and place in a clean bottle with the olive oil. Seal tightly and allow to stand in a cool place for 2 weeks.

## Rosemary

- 2-3 stems of fresh rosemary
- 2 cups extra virgin olive oil

Submerge rosemary in oil in a bottle. Seal tightly and allow to stand in a cool place for 2 weeks.

# Orange & Mustard Dressing

**Makes 1 cup**

- ¾ cup orange juice
- 1/3 cup mustard
- 1 cup olive oil

Whisk all ingredients together, season with sea salt and pepper and then enjoy!

# Poppy Seed Dressing

**Makes approx. ½ cup.  Inspired by Jodie Branche.**

- 1 tbs. poppy seeds
- 4 tbs. organic honey
- 4 tbs. macadamia nut oil

Put all ingredients in a squirt bottle or jar and shake.  Serve over salad. Store in fridge when not in use.

# Queenie's Mayonnaise

**Makes approx. 2 cups.  A recipe from Queenie Bermingham.**

- 380g can condensed milk
- 2 tsp. dry mustard
- ½ - ¾ cup white or brown vinegar

Pour condensed milk into a jar and add mustard stirring well.  Add ½ cup of vinegar and mix thoroughly.  Add remaining vinegar if needed.

# Raita

**Makes 2 cups**

- *1 cup plain yoghurt*
- *1 small cucumber*
- *1 tbs. chopped fresh mint*
- *1 small vine-ripened tomato, diced*

Mix all ingredients together and season well.

# Sweet Chilli Dressing

**Serves 4.  Recipe by Tracey Stevens.**

- *100mls olive oil*
- *1 tbs. whole grain mustard*
- *1 tbs. sweet chilli sauce*
- *1/3 cup white vinegar*

Combine all ingredients in a screw top jar and shake to combine.

*Optional:  Add a clove of garlic and 1 tsp. brown sugar.*

# Sauces

Success doesn't come to you ... You go to it!

**Unknown**

---

## Aioli

**A recipe from Bella Boo Cafe, Mundubbera QLD.**

- *½ cup whole egg mayonnaise*
- *1 tsp. crushed garlic*
- *2 tbs. lemon juice*

Mix all together, season with sea salt and pepper and chill for several hours before serving, allowing time for flavours to infuse.

*Optional: Add ½ tsp. mustard and 1 tsp. honey for a difference. Delicious served with almost any seafood dish.*

## Blue Cheese Butter

**Makes 1½ cups.  Recipe by Jan Neale.**

- *200g block blue cheese*
- *½ cup butter*
- *¼ cup finely chopped parsley*
- *1 tsp. lemon juice*

Process all ingredients in a food processor for 30 seconds or until well mixed.  Serve with warm, crusty French stick accompanying a pasta dish ... Yummy!

# Capsicum & Chive Butter

**Makes approx. 1 cup**

- *¼ cup well drained capsicum, diced*
- *1 tbs. chopped chives*
- *½ cup butter, softened*

Beat altogether and serve over warm corn on the cob.  Great at any BBQ.

# Cream Sauce

**Makes 1 cup.  Recipe by Gabrielle Bluett.**

- *1 cup thickened cream*
- *2 tsp. mustard*
- *1 tsp. horseradish (optional)*
- *1 tbs. lemon juice*

Place cream in a saucepan and heat through.  Remove from heat before adding all other ingredients and stirring well.

# Green Peppercorn Sauce

**Enough for 1**

- *1½ tsp. green peppercorns*
- *¼ cup pouring cream*

Add peppercorns to hot frying pan (if accompanying meat), add to the frying pan after cooking meat.  Reduce heat to medium. Cook, stirring, for 1 minute. Stir in cream.  Simmer for 2 minutes or until sauce thickens.  Delicious over steak served with baked potato and veges.

# Hollandaise Sauce

**Makes ¾ cup**

- 2 egg yolks
- ½ cup butter, melted
- 2 tbs. vinegar

Place egg yolks and 2 tbs. vinegar in a food processor whisking until blended. Add warm butter slowly until thick and creamy, season with a pinch of sea salt and cracked pepper. Serve warm over an English muffin with crispy bacon or salmon and a poached egg.

# Hot Fudge Sauce

**Makes 1 cup ... You'll wish it made more!**

- 200g dark chocolate, chopped
- 1 cup white marshmallows, chopped
- 1 cup cream

Combine all ingredients in a microwave dish and heat on high stirring every 30 seconds until blended.

*Optional: Serve drizzled over the peanut butter ice-cream pie, see: Desserts.*

# Lemon & Lime Reduction

**Makes 1 cup.  A recipe by Kelly Mauger, for any seafood dish.**

- *2 cups caster sugar*
- *2 whole lemons*
- *2 whole limes*
- *A sprinkle of chilli flakes*

Pour 2 cups of water into a saucepan along with sugar, lemons and limes and bring to the boil.  Reduce to a simmer for about 30 minutes.  Remove from heat and take out  whole lemons and limes, add chilli flakes to taste and allow to cool.

# Mint Sauce

**Makes a lovely glaze served over roast lamb.**

- *2 tbs. finely chopped mint*
- *2 tbs. lemon juice*
- *1 tbs. sugar*

Place all ingredients plus 4 tbs.  boiling water into a small saucepan and cook over a low heat for 5 minutes.  Allow to stand for 30 minutes before serving.

# Plum Sauce

**Makes ½ cup.  Recipe by Gabrielle Bluett.**

- *6 tsp. plum jam*
- *2 tsp. grated ginger*
- *2 tsp. sesame oil*
- *2 tbs. rice vinegar*

Mix all ingredients in a saucepan on a very low heat and serve warm.

# Salsa

**Makes 1 cup**

- *1 avocado, diced*
- *1 tsp. finely chopped red chilli*
- *Juice of ½ lime*
- *¼ cup diced red capsicum*

Combine altogether (may need a little more lime juice) and serve over grilled fish or pork.

*Hint: To maintain freshness of coriander; wrap it in a damp tea towel and refrigerate.*

# Satay Sauce

**Make ¼ cup.  Recipe by Gabrielle Bluett.**

- *2 tbs. crunchy peanut butter*
- *2tbs. Tamarind chilli sauce*
- *1 tbs. coconut milk powder*

Mix all ingredients well with ¼ cup of water and heat in a saucepan on a low heat.

# Cocktail Food

*"Choose your Attitude!"*

**Inside of a lift at Radio National, Auckland N.Z.**

## Asparagus Wraps

**A recipe from the gifted Kelly Mauger.  *Absolutely DIVINE!!!***

- *2 bunches asparagus, ends trimmed*
- *8 slices prosciutto*
- *2 tbs. extra virgin olive oil*

Preheat oven to 180C.  Use a sharp knife to cut the prosciutto lengthways into thin, long strips.  Wrap a piece of prosciutto around each asparagus spear, creating a long, spiral effect.  Place each spear on baking tray, drizzle with oil and season with sea salt and pepper.  Bake for 5-6 minutes.

## Baked Haloumi

**A recipe from Jane Saunders, Whangarei N.Z.**

- *250g pkt haloumi cheese, drained and cut into 3cm cubes*
- *2 tbs. plain flour*
- *3 tbs. extra virgin olive oil*
- *2 tbs. fresh lemon juice*

Place flour on small plate, season with sea salt and pepper and evenly coat haloumi.  Heat oil in non-stick frying pan over high heat.  Add haloumi and turn occasionally for 2 minutes or until golden brown.  Transfer to serving plate, sprinkle with lemon juice and season with pepper.

# Cheddar & Thyme Wafers

**Makes 10.  Recipe by Wendy King.**

- *2 cups grated tasty cheese*
- *1 cup shaved parmesan cheese*
- *10 sprigs fresh thyme*

Preheat oven to 180C.  Combine cheeses and on a baking paper lined tray, make 10 circles with cheeses, top with fresh thyme leaves.  Bake for 12-15 minutes until golden brown.  Remove from tray and place on absorbent paper to soak up excess oil.  After a couple of minutes coil cheese wafers over rolling pin or narrow glass to make curled shape.  Use wafers for dips or garnish for a salad.

# Cheese Triangles

**Makes 12.  Always a winner served with sweet chilli sauce to dip.**

- *500g Feta cheese*
- *375g filo pastry*
- *3 eggs, beaten*
- *½ cup melted butter*

Preheat oven 200C.  Crumble feta in a bowl and add eggs, combine well.  Remove 1 sheet of pastry and brush with melted butter.  Place second sheet on top and brush with butter, repeat with third sheet.  Cut pastry into 4 lengthwise (each of these 4 strips makes 1 triangle.)  Place 2 tsp. of cheese mixture onto edge of each strip.  Fold into a triangle and keep folding maintaining the triangle shape.  Place on a buttered (or paper lined) oven tray and bake at 200C for 20 minutes.

# Chipolata Rolls with Spicy Tomato Sauce

**Makes 8**

- *2 sheets frozen puff pastry*
- *500g pkt extra-lean chipolata sausages*
- *2/3 cup tomato sauce*
- *2 tbs. Worcestershire sauce*

Preheat oven to 220C. Cut pastry sheets into quarters. Wrap pastry around the centre of each sausage. Brush edges of pastry with water and press to seal. Place sausage rolls, seam down, on a baking tray. Bake for 18 minutes or until golden brown. Mix sauces together and serve with baked chipolata rolls.


# Creamy Brie

- *125g wheel of double brie cheese*
- *1 tbs. raspberry jam*
- *100g flaked almonds, toasted*

Place brie on a microwave safe serving plate, spread with jam and press on almonds to coat. Cook on high for 30 seconds, wait 5 seconds and repeat this process twice to prevent over heating the cheese. Serve with melba toast or your favourite cracker.

*Optional: Use whatever jam you like.*

# Curry Curls

**Makes 50.  A tasty delight from Joy Duke.**

- *250g packet potato chips, finely crushed*
- *2 tsp. curry powder*
- *4 sheets puff pastry*

Preheat oven to 180C.  Combine chips and curry powder in a bowl. Sprinkle one pastry sheet with mixture.  Place a sheet of pastry on top and press down firmly.  Repeat with remaining pastry and mixture. Cut into 2cm strips.  Twist to curl and bake on a paper lined baking tray for 15-20 minutes or until golden brown.


# Fried Calamari

**Serves 4.  *Y.u.m ... Y.u.m ... Y.u.m!!!***

- *4 fillets of whole fresh squid cleaned and cut into 2 cm rings or strips*
- *½ cup extra virgin olive oil*
- *3 cups plain organic flour*
- *¾ cup vegetable seasoning*

Pat squid dry with absorbent paper and heat oil in a large fry pan. Combine flour and seasoning, toss calamari through and shake excess off before frying quickly in very hot oil until tender (about 2 minutes).  Lay on paper to absorb excess oil and serve with a sprinkle of sea salt.

*Optional:  Divine served with Aioli.*

# Garlic Macadamias

- *2 cups macadamia nuts, unsalted*
- *Macadamia nut oil spray (or extra virgin olive oil spray)*
- *Garlic Salt*

Preheat oven to 180C. Tip the macadamia nuts onto a baking paper lined tray and spread so they are sitting on the tray evenly. Roast for 7-8 minutes. Remove, immediately spray with oil and sprinkle with garlic salt. Serve warm.


# Honey Roasted Peanuts

- *350g raw shelled peanuts*
- *½ cup honey*
- *1½ tsp. Chinese five spice powder*

Preheat oven to 150C. Combine ingredients in a small saucepan and warm over low heat. Spread nuts onto a large baking tray, lined with baking paper and bake for 15 minutes or until golden brown.


# Mini Roasted Capsicum Tartlets

**Makes 10**

- *1 sheet puff pastry, thawed*
- *250g tub roasted capsicum dip*
- *5 slices of char-grilled marinated capsicum, chopped coarsely*
- *¼ cup fresh basil leaves*

Preheat oven to 200C. Using a scone cutter cut 10 rounds into sheet of pastry. Line patty pan holes (may need greasing if not non-stick). Divide dip equally into rounds, top with capsicum and bake for 15 minutes. Remove, allow to cool slightly and top with fresh basil leaves. Serve warm.

# Mini Salmon Cream Quiche

**Makes 24**

- 2 x 150g tub smoked salmon cream cheese (at room temp.)
- ½ cup milk
- 3 eggs
- 2 sheets puff pastry

Cut 9 rounds with a scone cutter from each sheet of pastry, combine excess and roll to cut a further 6 rounds. Line a non-stick 12 hole patty cake tin. In a bowl or blender, mix first 3 ingredients. Pour mixture into each and bake in 180C oven for 30 minutes or until filling is puffed and pastry golden. Repeat the process for next 12. Allow to stand for 10 minutes before removing from tray.

*Optional: Season with pepper and top with a sprig of fresh dill or the zest of a lemon.*


# Olive Triangles

**Makes 16**

- 60g semi-dried tomatoes, chopped
- 100g pitted kalamata olives, chopped
- 1 sheet frozen puff pastry
- Extra virgin olive oil spray

Preheat oven to 200C. Lightly grease a baking tray. Combine olives and tomatoes and evenly spread the mixture over the pastry, pressing gently. Cut pastry into quarters and then again diagonally forming 4 triangles per quarter. Place onto tray and bake for 12 minutes or until crisp and golden.

*Optional: These are delicious served with hummus or your favourite dip.*

# Onions on Horseback

- *1 jar pickled onions*
- *3 slices of bacon, quartered*

Roll each pickled onion in a piece of bacon and fix securely with a toothpick. At serving time, grill until bacon is crisp or bake in a hot oven.

*Options:*

- *Devils on Horseback; replace the onion with a pitted prune*

- *Angels on Horseback; replace the onion with an oyster, season with salt, pepper and lemon juice.*


# Parmesan Shapes

**Makes 32. A recipe by Wendy King.**

- *2 sheets puff pastry, thawed*
- *½ cup finely grated Parmesan cheese*
- *Sprinkle of garlic salt*

Preheat oven to 180C. Line tray with baking paper then using a small cookie cutter cut out approx. 16 shapes from each pastry sheet. Sprinkle pastry with cheese and garlic salt then bake for 10-15 minutes until puffed and golden. Serve warm.

# Pesto Palmiers

**Makes 24**

- ½ cup basil pesto
- ¼ cup grated parmesan
- 2 sheets puff pastry, chilled

Spread each pastry sheet with basil and parmesan and season. Roll up one side until you reach the middle then repeat with the other side. Place both rolls on a paper lined baking tray and freeze for 30 minutes. Remove and slice each into 1½ cm slices. Bake in a 200C oven for 15-20 minutes, or until golden brown ...
*Watch them disappear.*

# Ricotta & Prosciutto Baked Pies

**Makes 12. A recipe from the vibrant Perditta O'Connor.**

- 5 slices prosciutto
- 400g fresh ricotta
- 6 sprigs fresh thyme, leaves picked
- 1 bunch chives, coarsely chopped

Preheat oven 180C. Line the base and interior of each mini-muffin pan with the prosciutto. Combine ricotta, thyme and chives in a bowl. Distribute mixture evenly into muffin section and bake for 15 minutes or until set. Remove tray and set aside for another 15 minutes to cool before serving.

*Optional: Season with sea salt and pepper and bake topped with some halved cherry tomatoes.*

# Spicy Cheddar Shortbread

**Makes approx. 50.  This one is great with drinks before dinner.**

- *2¼ cups plain flour*
- *250g butter, slightly softened (reserve just a little for greasing)*
- *1½ cups grated cheddar cheese*
- *¼ tsp. cayenne pepper*

Place all ingredients (except a ¼ cup plain flour) in a food processor or blender.  Process using pulse until just combined.  Turn out onto a floured surface (use remaining ¼ cup) and shape into a ball.  Cut in half and roll each half into a 30cm log about 3 cm in diameter.  Wrap in Glad Wrap.  Chill until firm (35 minutes).  Preheat oven 200C.  Lightly grease a baking tray cut logs into 5 mm thick rounds, place 2-3 cm apart and bake for 15-20 minutes until golden.  Cool completely.  Store in an airtight container.

*Optional:  Sprinkle with sesame seeds prior to baking.*

# Sunshine State Skewers

**Makes 48**

- *500g kabana, sliced into 2cm pieces*
- *½ fresh pineapple, chopped into chunks*
- *48 toothpicks*
- *1 jar ginger marmalade*

Thread kabana and pineapple pieces onto the toothpicks.  Glaze completely with ginger marmalade and grill or BBQ until sizzling.

*Optional:  A tin of chopped pineapple pieces can be substituted.*

# Tempting Mini-Pizzas

**Makes 12**

- *1 sheet puff pastry*
- *2 tbs. pizza sauce*
- *250g tub antipasto mix*
- *100g feta*

Using a scone cutter, cut 12 rounds into puff pastry. Place on a baking paper lined baking tray and brush with pizza sauce. Distribute evenly the antipasto mix and top with a slice of feta. Place in 180C oven for 15 minutes. Serve warm.

*Optional: Substitute pizza sauce with basil pesto, or mix both for an interesting change. Top with whatever you like.*

# Tuna Log

- *1 pkt. French onion soup*
- *150g tin tuna*
- *250g cream cheese, softened*
- *¼ cup sesame seeds*

Combine all ingredients except sesame seeds. Mould into a log and roll in seeds. Refrigerate before serving with crackers and a mezze of vege sticks.

# Morning & Afternoon Teas

Time is not measured by the years that you live
But by the deeds that you do, and the joy that you give!

**Anonymous**

---

## Amoretti Biscuits

**Makes 25. Recipe from Kate Schenk.**

- 2 cups almond meal
- 1 tsp. almond essence
- ¾ cup caster sugar
- 4 egg whites

Preheat oven to 130C. Combine meal and essence and about ¾ of the caster sugar. Beat the egg whites until stiff, adding the remaining caster sugar gradually. In three lots, fold almond meal into the beaten egg whites. Spoon into a piping bag with a large nozzle, (or plastic zip lock bag with ½ cm hole cut from one corner) and pipe walnut-sized pieces onto lined baking trays. Bake for 40 minutes.

## Another Caramel Treat

**Makes 36. *Soooo* easy and *soooo* yummy!**

- 200g Jersey caramels
- 1½ tbs. milk
- 2½ cups toasted muesli

In a saucepan over low heat melt caramels with milk stirring until smooth. Add in muesli, cool slightly. With a tsp. roll into balls, place on baking trays in the refrigerator to set. Damp hands will roll these easier.

---

# Apple Slice

**THIS WILL IMPRESS!**

- 340g pkt vanilla cake mix
- ¾ cup melted butter
- 400g tin pie apple
- 200g sour cream

Preheat oven to 180C. Mix butter and cake mix to a dough. Spread evenly in a paper lined rectangular baking dish and bake for 15 minutes. Combine apple and sour cream. Spread evenly over base and return to oven for another 15 minutes. Cool in the fridge. Serve cold.

*Optional: You can sprinkle with cinnamon before the final bake or use a tin of pie apple with cinnamon instead.*

# Biscuit Pastry

- 1 tbs. butter
- 1 egg, well beaten
- 1 tbs. sugar
- 1 cup self raising flour

Beat sugar and butter, add egg and mix, add flour and roll out for tarts.

# 1,1,1,1, Cake

**A recipe from the poetic Belinda Gillam ... *Defines fast & fabulous!***

- *1 cup coconut*
- *1 cup milk*
- *1 cup caster sugar*
- *1 cup self raising flour*

Place all ingredients in a bowl and mix.  Line a loaf tin with baking paper and pour mixture in.  Bake in a preheated 180C oven for 40 minutes.

*Optional:  Serve warm with butter or plain ... Deliciously simple!*


# Cream Cheese Scones

**Makes 6**

- *250g cream cheese*
- *½ cup soft butter*
- *1 cup self-raising flour*

Mix cream cheese and butter with a beater until combined.  Gradually add the flour beating slowly until blended.  Roll out, cut with a scone cutter, arrange so that each is touching the other on a paper lined baking tray, and bake in a 200C oven for 12-15 minutes or until golden brown.

*Optional:  For savoury, add some parmesan cheese or sun-dried tomatoes.  For sweet, bake as is top with fresh cream and jam or butter and golden syrup.*

# Cashew Cream

A recipe from Kim Morrison who says "This makes a delicious change from cream on cakes, pancakes and desserts!"

- *1 cup cashew nuts, unsalted*
- *3 oranges, peeled and chopped*
- *1 apple, cored and peeled*
- *1 tbs. honey*

Place all ingredients in blender. Process until smooth and creamy. Serve cold.


# Christmas Balls

Makes 40. A recipe from Margaret Tindale ... *Everyone loooves these.*

- *4 cups coconut*
- *380g tin condensed milk*
- *100g pkt red glace cherries, finely chopped*
- *Zest of 1 lemon*

Place coconut, condensed milk and zest in a bowl and mix well. Add cherries and stir until the pink of the cherries runs through the mixture. Using a tsp. roll mixture into balls and place on two paper lined baking trays approx. 3cm apart. Bake in a 180c oven for 12-15 minutes, swapping trays half way through, or until balls are lightly browned. Remove and cool before serving.

# Custard Creams

**Makes 32 or 16 doubled.  A favourite of the Beattie Family!**

- *1 cup softened butter*
- *½ cup icing sugar*
- *1½ cups plain flour*
- *½ cup custard powder*

Preheat oven to 150C.  Beat butter and sugar to a cream.  Sift flour and custard powder together and gradually add to butter and sugar. Although crumbly, the mixture will roll into balls.  Place on paper lined baking tray.  Press lightly on each biscuit with a floured fork. Bake for 10 minutes or until pale golden colour.

*Optional:  Join together with lemon or passionfruit icing.*


# Date Scones

**Makes 12.  A recipe from Jennette McCosker.**

- *1 cup chopped dates*
- *300ml cream*
- *4 cups self raising flour (plus extra for rolling)*
- *375ml can ginger ale*

Preheat oven to 200C.  Sift flour into bowl, add remaining ingredients and stir until combined.  Place on floured surface and pat into a round shape about an inch thick.  Cut with scone cutter, arrange closely on a baking tray, and bake for 12-15 minutes or until golden brown.  Can be frozen or for a smaller quantity, simply halve the ingredients.

*Hint:  When making scones you can add 2 tbs. cornflour and a generous squeeze of lemon juice.  The cornflour will make the scones lighter and the lemon juice will keep them fresher for longer.*

# Date Loaf

**A recipe from Mrs. Frasier, Raceview QLD.  *Absolutely heavenly!***

- *375g pkt dates*
- *2 tsp. instant coffee*
- *1 cup self raising flour*
- *¼ cup flaked almonds*

Add coffee to 1 cup of boiling water and mix.  Pour over dates and soak overnight.  Stir in flour.  Pour mixture into a paper lined loaf tin, sprinkle with flaked almonds and bake in a preheated 160C oven for 45 minutes.

*Optional:  Serve warm with lashings of butter.*

# Easy Fruit Slice

**The same recipe submitted by both Maureen Wall and John Sealy ... Tis a goodie!**

- *380g tin condensed milk*
- *375g mixed fruit*
- *1 large cup self raising flour*

Preheat oven to 160C.  Mix all ingredients together and pour into a baking paper lined baking tray.  Bake for 40-45 minutes or until cooked when tested.  Allow to cool and slice.  Can be kept in freezer for up to one month.

*Optional:  For a flavour variation add one cup of coconut to the mixture before baking.  This is lovely served topped with lemon icing.*

# Fruit Bran Loaf

- *1 cup All-bran*
- *1 cup mixed dried fruit*
- *1½ cups milk*
- *1 cup self raising flour*

Preheat oven to 180C.  Combine bran, mixed fruit and milk in a bowl, stand for 15 minutes.  Add flour and mix well until combined.  Spoon mixture into a paper lined loaf tin and bake for 40 minutes or until cooked through.  Allow to cool in tin then turn out onto wire rack for further cooling.  Serve sliced.


# Fruity Cheese Tarts

**Makes 24**

- *1½ sheets shortcrust pastry,*
  *cut into 16 and 8 squares respectively*
- *250g cream cheese, softened*
- *¼ cup caster sugar*
- *1½ cups mixed fruit*

Line non-stick mini muffin tray with pastry, bake in 180C oven for 8 minutes or until crusts begin to brown.  Combine cheese and sugar, stir in mixed fruit, spoon into cooled shells.  Refrigerate for at least ½ hour before serving.

*Optional:  Decorate with a slice of fresh fruit.*

# Fruit Damper (an Australia day special)

**A little ripper from Joy Duke.**

- *375ml stubby of beer (can be heavy or light)*
- *2 cups mixed fruit*
- *3 cups self raising flour*
- *1 level tsp. salt*

Preheat oven to 180C.  Mix all ingredients together (like scone dough).  Place in paper lined oven dish (or loaf tin).  Bake for 30 minutes or  until top is golden brown and crispy.  Test with a knife.

*Optional:  Serve hot or cold with lashings of butter, golden syrup or jam.*

# Lemon Icing

**A recipe from the beautiful Wendy Beattie.**

- *2 tbs. butter*
- *½ cup icing sugar (may need a little extra)*
- *1 tsp. lemon juice*

Combine altogether ... How easy is that!

*Hint:  If your icing sugar becomes lumpy, remove lumps with rolling pin while still in packet, sift, then store in a tightly sealed container in the refrigerator.*

# Mock Cream # 1

**A recipe from the beautiful Jennette McCosker.**

- *1 cup icing sugar*
- *2 tbs. butter*
- *1 tbs. milk*
- *¼ tsp. vanilla essence*

Combine all ingredients and beat until light and fluffy.

# Mock Cream # 2

- *½ cup caster sugar*
- *½ cup butter*
- *1 tsp. vanilla essence*

Combine a third of a cup of water and sugar in a saucepan, stir consistently over heat until sugar is dissolved, then increase heat to bring to boil, remove from heat and allow to become completely cold. Beat butter and vanilla until white and fluffy gradually pouring in cold syrup beating constantly.

# Mouth Watering Mini-Cheesecakes

**Makes 55. These are fantastic, a new Bermingham favourite!
And you can freeze some for later (if there's any left!!!)**

- *1 pkt Oreos or chocolate/cream biscuits*
- *250g cream cheese*
- *380g tin condensed milk*
- *1 sachet gelatine*

Add 2 tbs. of condensed milk to the Oreo biscuits and blend until completely crushed and mixed. Spoon 1 tbs. of the mixture into the base of a silicon mini-muffin tray. Blend cream cheese and condensed milk until smooth. Mix gelatine with 3 tbs. of boiling water and add to cream cheese mix, stir thoroughly. Spoon mixture into muffin trays to cover the biscuit bases and refrigerate till set.

*Optional: Serve as is or topped with a sliver of strawberry, kiwi fruit, peach or dollop of raspberry sauce.*


# My Honey Icing

- *125g butter, softened*
- *¾ cup icing sugar*
- *1 tbs. milk*
- *¼ cup honey*

Beat all ingredients together until light and fluffy.

# Peanut Crisps

**Makes 16-20.  A recipe from the beautiful Lorraine Leeson.**

- *1 cup condensed milk*
- *½ cup peanut paste*
- *3 cups cornflakes*

Combine condensed milk and peanut paste before adding cornflakes.  Place spoonfuls on a paper lined oven tray and bake in 180C oven for 15-20 minutes.


**A variation from Joy Duke, makes 40.**

- *380g can condensed milk*
- *½ cup peanut butter*
- *3 cups desiccated coconut*
- *1 cup chopped nuts, unsalted*

Preheat oven to 180C.  Mix condensed milk and peanut butter thoroughly.  Stir in coconut and nuts.  Drop heaped tsp. onto paper lined oven trays.  Bake for 15 minutes, or until golden brown.

# Pear Cake

**Makes 8. A recipe from the adorable Brett McCosker ... Very easy and very nice!**

- *400g can pears*
- *340g pkt vanilla cake mix*
- *3 eggs*

Preheat oven to 180C. Drain pears, reserving the liquid. Place pears and liquid into a mixing bowl, add cake mix, 2 egg whites and 1 whole egg. Beat on low speed for 30 seconds, then on high for 4 minutes. Pour mixture into a paper lined 22cm cake tin and bake for 55 minutes or until inserted skewer comes out clean.

*Optional: Delectable served with mock cream and sprinkled with coconut.*

# Pikelets

**Makes 10**

- *1 egg*
- *1 cup self raising flour*
- *4 tsp. sugar*
- *½ cup milk*

Beat egg and sugar together before adding the other ingredients, mix thoroughly. Heat a non-stick frypan and dollop a heaped tbs. of the mixture into it. Flip pikelet when you see small bubbles forming on its upper side. Cook for a further minute and repeat until the mixture is used. Serve with butter, cream, jam, fruit or syrup.

# Pineapple Tart

**Recipe by Joy Duke, a birthday favourite of her children.**

- *400g can crushed pineapple*
- *¼ cup custard powder*
- *1½ cups milk*
- *1 sheet shortcrust pastry*

Place pastry in a tart dish and bake in a 180C oven for 10–12 minutes or until lightly golden, remove and cool. Gently boil crushed pineapple in saucepan. Combine custard powder and milk and add to crushed pineapple. Stir until thick (10–15 minutes) and pour into pastry shell, allow to cool and set for 2 hours.

*Optional: Decorate with fresh whipped cream and crumbled flake or fresh fruit.*

# Raisin Loaf

**A recipe from the quirky Kt Anbeck ... *Yummy!***

- *1 tbs. butter (a little extra for greasing)*
- *1 cup sugar*
- *1 cup raisins*
- *2 cups self raising flour*

Preheat oven to 180C. Place butter, sugar and raisins in a saucepan with 1 cup water and bring to boil. Reduce heat and simmer for 5 minutes, set aside and allow to cool. Add flour and mix well. Bake in a greased loaf tin for 45 minutes.

*Optional: Cut into thick slices and serve with butter.*

# Savoury Scones

**Makes 12. This clever recipe was learnt at a 612 ABC Brisbane Breakfast Radio interview - *Thanks Majella!***

- *4 cups self raising flour*
- *300ml cream*
- *375ml bottle soda water*
- *½ cup semi-dried tomatoes, chopped*

Sift self raising flour into a bowl, make a well and pour in cream and soda water then add tomatoes and season. Mix to make a firm dough, roll out and cut with a scone cutter. Place on a paper lined baking tray so that the scones are touching and bake in a 200C oven until golden brown.

*Optional: Sprinkle with parmesan cheese before baking. Substitute tomatoes with capers, bacon, olives, corn, fresh herbs or whatever you like.*

# Spicy Fruit Mince Tarts

**Makes 12. You'll be surprised and delighted!**

- *6 slices raisin bread, crusts removed*
- *2 tbs. butter*
- *A jar of your favourite fruit mince*

Butter bread on both sides and cut rounds large enough to line a muffin tray. Cook in a 180C oven for 3-5 minutes, remove and fill with fruit mince, return to oven for 5 minutes or until edges of bread are a light golden brown.

*Optional: Dust with icing sugar or a dollop of whipped cream for serving.*

# Sponge Cake

**A second generation recipe from Jill McIver.**

- *4 eggs (room temperature)*
- *¾ cup caster sugar*
- *¾ cup self raising flour, sifted 5 times*
- *Dash vanilla essence*

Preheat oven to 210C. Beat eggs and sugar with an electric beater for 15 minutes, add vanilla just before beating completes. Gently fold in flour with a spatula until combined. Line a lamington tin with baking paper and place in oven, bake for approx. 14 minutes. Remove, cool, cut in half and serve with jam and freshly whipped cream either as a single layer or double.

*Hint: During the cooking of a cake, if the top starts to over-brown, cover loosely with alfoil.*


# Vanilla Slice

**A s.c.r.u.m.p.t.i.o.u.s recipe from the delightful Val Savage.**

- *1 pkt lattice biscuits*
- *600ml cream*
- *1 pkt vanilla instant pudding*

Place a layer of biscuits on the bottom of a baking dish. Mix cream and pudding together until thick, pour onto biscuit base and top with another layer of lattice bickies.

*Optional: When in season, add 2 fresh mangoes peeled and sliced to the mixture. Top with the following icing.*

# Passionfruit Icing

- *1 cup icing sugar*
- *1 passionfruit pulp*
- *1 tsp. butter, softened*

Mix all ingredients well.

# 1,2,3,4 Cake

**A recipe by from the lovely Tanya Ormsby.**

- *1 cup butter*
- *2 cups sugar*
- *3 cups self raising flour*
- *4 eggs*

Preheat oven to 140C. Grease a 22cm spring form cake tin. Using an electric mixer, cream butter and sugar for 5 minutes or until pale and fluffy. Add eggs one at a time, beating well between each addition. Fold through sifted flour. Spoon into prepared pan and bake for 1¼ hours (cover with alfoil if cake is browning too quickly). Cool in tin before turning out.

*Optional: Delicious topped with a layer of freshly whipped cream and fresh strawberries.*

# Versatile Fruit Cake

**A recipe by the lovely Mai Spoor.**

- *400ml tin coconut milk*
- *375g pkt mixed fruit*
- *1 cup self raising flour*

Soak fruit in coconut milk overnight. Add self raising flour and mix well. Bake in a paper lined loaf tin on 125C for approx. 2 hours or until cooked through.

**A recipe by the effervescent Royelle McDonald.**

- *600ml chocolate Breaka*
- *1kg mixed fruit*
- *2 large cups self raising flour*

Soak fruit in milk overnight. Add self raising flour and mix well. Bake in a paper lined cake tin on 125C for approx. 2-2½ hours or until cooked through.

**A recipe by Joy Duke.**

- *450g tin mangoes*
- *1kg mixed fruit*
- *2 cups self raising flour*

Soak fruit in mango juice and chopped flesh overnight. Add self raising flour and mix well. Bake in a paper lined cake tin on 125C for approx. 2-2½ hours or until cooked through.

**Glen Turnbull's favourite Fruit Cake, recipe from Sr. Jeanette Collis.**

- *1kg mixed fruit*
- *2 tbs. instant coffee*
- *150g block fruit and nut chocolate, roughly chopped*
- *2 cups self raising flour*

Make 2 cups coffee with instant coffee and boiling water, add to fruit and soak overnight. Add chocolate and flour and mix well. Bake in a paper lined cake tin on 125C for approx. 2-2½ hours or until cooked through.

# Light Meals & Lunches

The trouble with a diet
is often you don't eat what you like,
and don't like what you eat.

**An unsuccessful dieter!!!!**

---

# Soups

## Bacon & Pea Soup

**Serves 4-6.  This is really tasty!**

- *1 kg bacon bones*
- *200g pkt dried peas*
- *2 onions, roughly chopped*

Place all ingredients in a large saucepan with 10 cups water.  Bring to boil and then simmer for 1 hour.  Remove from heat and allow to cool.  Remove bacon from bones.  If soup is too thick add more water.  Blend and serve with a crusty French loaf.

## Cauliflower Soup

**Serves 4-6.  A recipe from Jennette McCosker.**

- *A small fresh cauliflower*
- *300ml tub cream*
- *1 tbs. oyster sauce*

Place chopped cauliflower in a saucepan with 2 cups water and cook until tender.  Allow to cool before blending.  Mix in cream and oyster sauce and season well.  Serve warm.

# Chorizo & Capsicum Soup

**This serves 6-8 and is REALLLLLLLY TASTY!**

- *2 chorizo sausages, diced*
- *4 red capsicums, diced*
- *410g tin whole peeled tomatoes*
- *750ml chicken stock*

Fry chorizo in a non-stick pan for 5 minutes, remove from pan and set aside. Into the same pan with chorizo juices add capsicum and fry for 5 minutes before adding tomatoes. Mix well, season with sea salt and pepper, add stock and bring to boil. Reduce heat and simmer until capsicums are tender. Puree the soup and serve with chorizo pieces.

# Parmesan Crisps

**Makes 6. A recipe by Lorraine Leeson.**

- *200g wedge parmesan cheese*
- *1 tbs. sesame seeds*

Preheat oven to 200C. Line a tray with baking paper and place 6 egg rings on top. Into each, thinly grate enough parmesan to cover the base. Top with a sprinkle of sesame seeds, gently remove egg rings and bake for 8 minutes or until the cheese melts into lacey discs. Allow to cool and serve with your favourite soup or as a nibble with drinks.

*Optional: Substitute sesame seeds with a sprinkle of smokey paprika or a smattering of your favourite fresh herb.*

# Pumpkin, Lentil & Ginger Soup

**Serves 4**

- ½ cup red lentils, rinsed
- 1kg butternut pumpkin, cut into chunks
- 1 tbs. grated ginger
- 4 cups vegetable stock

Place all ingredients into a large saucepan, season with sea salt and pepper if you like and cook on a medium heat cook for 30 minutes. Blend and serve.


# Qld Blue Pumpkin Soup

**Serves 4**

- 1 kg pumpkin, peeled and chopped
- 1 generous tsp. curry powder
- 1 clove garlic
- 150ml thickened cream

Place pumpkin, curry and garlic in a saucepan and add 2 cups of water. Season with sea salt and pepper if you like, bring to boil then reduce heat and simmer for 20 minutes or until pumpkin is tender. Blend before adding cream, stir through and serve.

*Hint:  Give plain pumpkin soup a lift by stirring in a ¼ cup crunchy peanut butter and a handful of chopped coriander to each litre of soup.*

# Smoked Salmon & Corn Chowder

**Serves 6.  A recipe from the lovely Katrina Price.**

- *6 cups fish stock*
- *400g white sweet potato, peeled and chopped*
- *225g can creamed corn*
- *350g can smoked salmon*

Place stock and potato in a saucepan and bring to boil, reduce heat and simmer until potato is cooked.  Add salmon and corn and continue to simmer for 5 minutes then blend until smooth.  Serve warm.

# Sweet Potato Soup

**Serves 4.  A recipe from Rebecca Butler.**

- *2 cups chicken stock*
- *½ cup finely chopped onion*
- *2 cups mashed sweet potato*
- *¼ cup sour cream*

Over a low heat, cook onion in a non-stick pan until golden.  Add stock and mash and bring to the boil, stirring until nice and smooth.  Reduce heat and simmer for 10 minutes, add sour cream with a few minutes remaining.

*Optional:  Garnish with fresh coriander and season to taste.  Chicken stock can be replaced with vegetable stock.*

# Tomato Soup

**Serves 4.  Recipe from Michelle Dodd "Light & Licious!!!"**

- *16 Roma tomatoes*
- *2 tbs. extra virgin olive oil*
- *4 sprigs fresh thyme*
- *4 cups of vegetable stock*

Slice tomatoes in half, place on an alfoil lined baking tray cut side up and drizzle with oil.  Season with sea salt, pepper and thyme.  Bake in a 180C oven for 40 minutes.  Remove and allow to cool slightly.  Blend tomatoes and vege stock, pour through a sieve to remove seeds and into a saucepan to simmer for 15 minutes.  Serve warm with fresh, crusty bread.

# Vegetable Croutons

**Serves 4.  A recipe by Lorraine Leeson.**

- *¼ cup extra virgin olive oil*
- *1 small sweet potato or parsnip, peeled and diced*
- *1 clove garlic*

Heat oil in a large pan.  Add the vegetables and garlic and cook for 10 minutes or until tender and lightly browned.  Drain on paper and sprinkle over soup.

*Hint:  If any of your hot soups end up slightly salty, add to it a whole, peeled potato and simmer for about 15 minutes to absorb salt.  Remove the potato and serve.*

# All Others

*"Everything has its beauty, but not everyone sees it."*

**Confucius**

---

## Banana & Bacon Melt

**Serves 2.  A recipe by Marg Morters, Central Coast NSW.**

- *2 bacon rashers*
- *4 slices wholemeal bread*
- *1 large banana*
- *½ cup grated tasty cheese*

Crisp fry some bacon. Toast bread under grill on one side only. Slice banana length ways and place on untoasted side of bread with a couple of bits of cooked bacon. Top with grated cheese and place under hot grill until cheese has melted and is bubbly.

*Optional:  Cut into fingers before serving.*

*Topping Options:*

- *Bacon, pineapple and cheese*
- *Ham, corn, pineapple and cheese*
- *Chicken, asparagus and cheese*
- *Chicken, semi-dried tomatoes and feta*
- *Chicken, avocado and cheese*
- *Ham, asparagus, pineapple and cheese*
- *Salami, antipasto and cheese*

# BBQ Chicken Burgers

**Makes 4**

- *½ cooked BBQ chicken, finely chopped*
- *1 cup wholegrain breadcrumbs*
- *½ cup sour cream (may need a little more)*
- *4 hamburger buns*

Preheat oven to 180C.  Mix chicken, breadcrumbs and sour cream together and season with sea salt and pepper.  Roll into patties and bake in a 180C oven for 20 minutes.  Serve in buns with lots of salad and BBQ sauce.

*Optional:  Place on a hot BBQ with a little olive oil and cook for 4 minutes or until golden brown then flip and cook for a further 3 minutes.*


# BBQ Chicken Pizza

**Makes 1.  Recipe from Rodger Fishwick.**

- *1 pita pocket*
- *1-2 tbs. BBQ sauce*
- *½ cup BBQ chicken*
- *¼ cup mozzarella cheese*

Preheat oven to 180C.  Take a pita pocket and spread BBQ sauce evenly over the top.  Add chicken and sprinkle with mozzarella cheese.  Place on alfoil lined baking tray and bake for 10 minutes.

# Chicken Nachos

**Serves 6. A sensational footy nibble that everyone can enjoy ...
Just ask Paul Bermingham.**

- *1 large pkt plain corn chips*
- *2½ cups grated cheese*
- *2 cups cooked chicken, pulled apart into small pieces*
- *2 tbs. BBQ sauce or sweet chilli sauce*

Spread a layer of corn chips on an oven-proof plate. Sprinkle with chicken and cheese followed by a squirt of sauce. Continue process until chicken is all gone and end with ½ cup of cheese. Put in oven for 10 minutes to melt cheese and serve. Can also melt in microwave.

*Optional: Top with Guacamole – Yum!!!*

# Cheese Panini

- *2 slices panini bread*
- *2 slices Swiss cheese*
- *1 tomato, sliced*
- *1 sprig thyme, finely chopped*

Toast Panini and immediately place cheese on top. Top with tomato and sprinkle with some thyme and serve.

# Chicken Vol-Au-Vonts

**Serves 4**

- *4 large vol-au-vont shells*
- *485g bottle Chicken Tonight, honey mustard*
- *1 cup shredded cheese*
- *2 double chicken breast fillets, diced*

Preheat oven to 180C. Dice chicken and cook in a non-stick fry pan till lightly browned. Turn down heat and add chicken tonight, stir to heat through. Place vol-au-vont shells on a lined baking tray and fill each with chicken mixture. Top with cheese and place in oven for 15 minutes or until cheese has bubbled and melted. Serve with salad or vegetables of choice.

*Optional: Cut 10 rounds from 2 sheets of puff pastry and blind bake instead of using vol-au-vent shells.*

# Curried Tuna Rollups

**Serves 4**

- *14 slices wholemeal bread, crusts removed*
- *1 cup grated cheese*
- *1 tsp. curry powder*
- *200g tin tuna chunks*

Preheat oven to 180C. Roll bread with a rolling pin to flatten. Combine remaining ingredients and spread on bread, roll and secure with toothpicks. Place rolls on a baking tray and bake for 15 minutes. Cut each roll in half and serve hot.

*Optional: ½ cup softened butter can be used instead of cheese. Brush rolls with melted butter before cooking for a golden brown finish.*

# Curry Pies

**Serves 4.  Fast and Fabulous!**

- *8 slices of wholegrain bread, crusts removed*
- *¼ cup milk*
- *400g can sweet curry (or your favourite curry)*

Roll bread with a rolling pin to flatten.  Use a teacup to cut a round shape from each slice and press into non-stick muffin tin.  Brush with milk and bake in a 180C oven until crisp and golden.  Heat sweet curry and spoon into cases.  Serve immediately.

*Optional:  Add in small pieces of leftover chicken, roast meat or veges.*

*Hint:  Grate excess bread to use as bread crumbs.*


# Ham & Cheese Muffins

**Makes 12.  A recipe from Lisa Logan.**

- *250g grated cheese*
- *2 cups self raising flour*
- *1½ cups milk*
- *½ cup chopped ham slices*

Sift flour and make a well in the middle, pour in milk, cheese and two thirds of the chopped ham.  Mix until combined.  Spoon into 12 large muffin tins and place a little of the remaining chopped ham on top of each one.  Bake at 180C for 25minutes until tops are golden brown.

*Optional:  These can be frozen.*

# Hot Salmon Puffs

**Makes 8**

- *2 sheets puff pastry, thawed*
- *220g can red salmon, drained*
- *4 shallots, finely chopped*
- *1/3 cup cream*

Place salmon, shallots and cream in a saucepan stirring over low heat until thickened. Season with pepper and stand until cool. Cut each sheet of pastry into quarters and evenly distribute the mixture to a corner. Fold into triangles firmly sealing the edges with a fork. Sprinkle each with water. Place the triangles on a lined baking tray and bake in a 180C oven until nicely browned.

# Mexican Style Stuffed Jacket Potatoes

**Makes 4**

- *4 potatoes, scrubbed*
- *½ cup taco sauce*
- *½ cup sour cream*
- *1 avocado, mashed*

Pierce each potato several times, wrap in alfoil and bake in 180C oven for 1 hour. Remove, and allow to cool before making a large crisscross slit in each. Divide sauce, cream and avocado among the potatoes and serve.

# Picnic Loaf

**A recipe from Michelle Dodd ... Yummo!**

- *1 Ciabatta loaf (Italian style bread with a hard crust)*
- *1 jar antipasto mix, drained*
- *1 small tub boccocini cheese, sliced*
- *Your choice of salami, ham, roasted sweet potato*

Cut the ciabatta loaf in half lengthways. Scoop out the bread. Fill one side with the antipasto. Fill the other side with bocconcini, follow with your choice of ham, salami or roasted sweet potato. Place the halves back together, wrap in baking paper and secure the paper with sticky tape. Pop in the fridge with a weight on top eg., an oblong casserole dish, and leave for 2-3 hours, or overnight if possible. To serve, unwrap and cut into slices.

# Prawn Cocktail

**Serves 4**

- *16 prawns peeled, de-veined and cooked*
- *2 tbs. mayonnaise*
- *2 tbs. tomato paste*
- *Juice of 1 lemon*

Place prawns in a margarita or large wine glass (a bread plate will also suffice). Mix mayonnaise, tomato paste and lemon juice together and pour over prawns and serve chilled.

*Optional: Serve with crispy fresh lettuce.*

# Salmon Pizza

**Makes 5**

- 5 small round pita breads
- 5 tbs. basil pesto
- 415g can red salmon, drained and flaked
- 10 bocconcini rounds, halved

Spread pita with 1 tbs. of pesto, top with salmon and bocconcini. Cook in a preheated 200C oven for 10 minutes.

*Optional:  Scatter each pizza with rocket to serve.*

# Satay Beef Pizza

**Makes 1.  Recipe from Rodger Fishwick.**

- 1 Turkish or pita bread
- 1tbs. Satay sauce
- ½ cup cooked mince
- ½ cup Mozzarella cheese

Preheat oven to 180C.  Cook mince in a non-stick frypan and place aside.  Place Turkish bread on a baking paper lined tray.  Spread satay sauce over base, top with mince and sprinkle with cheese. Bake for 10 minutes or until cheese has browned.

# Sausage Rolls

**Makes 12**

- *6 slices of bread*
- *2 tbs. butter*
- *3 thin pork sausages*

Remove crusts from bread and with rolling pin roll until quite smooth. Boil sausages until partly cooked, approx. 6 minutes and allow to cool. Butter each slice of bread right to the edges, cut sausage in half and roll firmly in the bread, securing with two toothpicks. Cut in half and bake in 180C oven on an alfoil lined tray until nicely browned.


# Savoury Butter

**Makes ¼ cup**

- *¼ cup butter, softened*
- *1 tbs. lemon juice*
- *Pinch celery salt*
- *Pinch cayenne pepper*

Mix all ingredients together and serve.


# Savoury Cases

**Makes 10. The idea for the following stems from the clever Daphne Beutel.**

- *10 slices of bread*
- *2 tbs. butter*

Remove crusts and butter bread both sides. Press each slice into a muffin tray. Bake in 180C oven for 5 minutes or until golden.

*Optional: These may be cooled and stored in airtight containers until required. To reheat, simply place in hot oven for a few minutes.*

# Savoury Case Asparagus Filling

- *1 pkt white sauce*
- *1½ cups milk*
- *220g tin asparagus pieces*
- *1 lemon*

Make the white sauce as per instructions using milk. Drain asparagus and mash with fork, then add to white sauce. Season with sea salt and pepper and serve in savoury cases topped with a generous amount of lemon zest.


# Savoury Case Curried Prawn Filling

- *1 pkt white sauce*
- *1½ cups milk*
- *1 tps. curry powder*
- *12 medium green prawns*

Make the white sauce as per instructions using milk and then add curry powder. Chop prawns and add to the sauce, stir until prawns are cooked.


# Savoury Case Salmon Filling

- *1 pkt white sauce*
- *1½ cups milk*
- *220g tin salmon*
- *1 tbs. finely chopped dill*

Make the white sauce as per instructions using milk. Drain salmon and mash with fork, then add it and dill to the white sauce. Season with pepper.

# Steak & Onion Pies

**Serves 4.  Kim's Dad, Errol McCosker's favourite!**

- *6 slices of bread*
- *2 tbs. butter*
- *420g can braised steak and onion*

Preheat oven to 180C.  Remove crusts and roll bread slices with a rolling pin.  Lightly butter both sides and cut as many circles as possible with a scone cutter.  Place in a greased patty tin, fill with steak and onion and place another bread circle on top of steak and onion.  Use a fork to seal the buttered bread together.  Pierce hole in the lid and bake for 10-12 minutes or until the lid is nicely browned.

# Sushi

- *1 cup of sushi rice or short grain rice*
- *2 tbs. Japanese rice vinegar*
- *2 sheets of Nori (or seaweed paper)*
- *½ avocado*

Preheat oven to 190C.  Wash rice and place into a casserole dish with 2 cups of water, cover and cook for 25 minutes, set aside for 10 minutes, mix through vinegar.  Place  some baking paper on a flat surface and lay a sheet of Nori (shiny side down) on top of it.  Wet hands and spread a thin layer of rice evenly so you can still see 1 cm of Nori around circumference.  Lay the avocado in the middle of the Nori going from one side to the other, horizontally.  Roll the sushi away from you keeping the roll firm. Damp the lip of the Nori before rolling it over fully and seal just as you would an envelope.  Roll in Glad Wrap and leave to stand for 10 minutes before cutting so sushi sets.  Sushi is best served freshly made.

*Optional:  Can also use other fillings such as cucumber, asparagus, bean sprouts, shredded carrots, salmon, chicken, ginger, prawns, caviar.  Serve with soy sauce and even wasabi if you like.*

# Sides

"Whatever you are, be a good one."

**Abraham Lincoln**

---

## Salads

### Carrot, Sultana & Celery Salad

**Serves 6**

- *4 cups grated carrot*
- *1 cup sultanas*
- *1½ cups thinly sliced celery*
- *¼ cup whole egg mayonnaise*

Mix all ingredients together and chill before serving.

*Optional:  Substitute celery for fresh pineapple.*

### Feta & Watermelon Salad

- *½ watermelon*
- *2 tbs. mint leaves, finely chopped*
- *1 Spanish onion, finely chopped*
- *50g feta cheese*

Cut watermelon into chunky cubes and remove seeds.  Add onion and mint and mix.  When ready to serve drain excess juice and place in a serving bowl.  Sprinkle with feta cheese.

*Optional:  Serve with caramelised balsamic vinegar.*

# Feta & Beetroot Salad

- *1 cup crumbled feta*
- *1 cup diced beetroot*
- *1 bag salad mix*
- *2 tbs. caramelised balsamic vinegar*

Combine first 3 ingredients and drizzle with the fourth.


# Garlic Pita Bread

**Serves 4. This is a lighter option for use as a side dish instead of garlic bread.**

- *2 slices pita bread*
- *2 tsp. butter*
- *2 tsp. crushed garlic*

Preheat oven to 180C.  Mix butter with garlic and spread liberally over each pita bread.  Cut into pie or wedge sized slices and place on lined baking tray.  Bake for 10 minutes or until just crisp.


# Mandarin Salad

**Serves 4-6. Inspired by 'the best dancer ever' Neville McCosker.**

- *½ iceberg lettuce*
- *3 mandarins, peeled*
- *2 avocados, peeled and sliced*
- *1 small Spanish onion, thinly sliced*

Shred lettuce and add remaining ingredients.  Cover and chill before serving with your favourite salad dressing.

# Octopus Salad

**Serves 4**

- *1 kg baby octopus, cleaned*
- *¾ cup balsamic salad dressing*
- *2 Lebanese cucumbers*
- *100g snow peas, trimmed*

Place octopus and salad dressing in a bowl, marinate for at least 1 hour. Preheat a non-stick frying pan until really hot. Cook undrained octopus in batches, turning frequently for 5 minutes until tender and slightly charred. Mount onto nests of cucumber and peas. Serve at once.

*Optional: Add ½ tsp. dried oregano to marinade.*

# Pasta Salad

**Serves 6. A recipe by Kate Macdonald.**

- *500g pkt tri-colour pasta spirals*
- *190g jar basil pesto*
- *1 small red onion, finely chopped*
- *½ cup pine nuts, toasted*

Cook the pasta according to packet directions. Once cooked, drain, rinse and allow to cool. Place in a serving bowl, mix through remaining ingredients and serve cold.

*Optional: You could use ordinary pasta but the tri-colour is really pretty!*

# Pea & Mint Salad

**Serves 4**

- *2 cups mixed frozen baby peas, snow peas etc.*
- *2 tbs. fresh mint, chopped*
- *1 cup feta cheese, crumbled*
- *2 tbs. fresh lemon juice*

Place peas in a serving dish and allow to sit in boiling water for 2 minutes. Drain and rinse under cold water, allow to dry. Add mint and feta. Drizzle with juice and toss gently to combine.

# Pushkin's Salad

**Serves 4. Recipe from 'Babushka' via Kent & Olya.**

- *4 carrots, grated*
- *3 cloves garlic, crushed*
- *½ cup walnuts, chopped*
- *4 tbs. mayonnaise*

Mix all ingredients together and serve. Substitute carrots for beetroots.

# Prawn and Mango Salad

**Serves 4**

- *12 large peeled, de-veined and cooked prawns*
- *1 large mango, peeled and sliced*
- *1 cucumber, sliced finely and length ways*
- *1 cup roasted cashews, unsalted*

Mix all ingredients lightly and serve. Quick, easy and delicious!

# Rocket & Parmesan Salad

**Serves 4. A recipe from the clever Cheyne McCorkindale.**

- *120g pkt baby rocket*
- *1-2 tbs. extra virgin olive oil*
- *½ Spanish onion, finely sliced*
- *¼ cup finely grated parmesan cheese*

Combine rocket and oil in a serving bowl. Add onions and parmesan and mix well, ensuring an even coating of parmesan across the rocket. Serve and enjoy!


# Spanish Orange Salad

**A recipe from Jennette McCosker.**

- *½ iceberg lettuce*
- *2 oranges, peeled and sliced*
- *½ Spanish onion, thinly sliced*

Arrange lettuce on serving plate and top with sliced oranges and onions. Serve with your favourite dressing.


# Speedy Potato Salad

**Serves 6. A recipe from Jan Neale.**

- *4 potatoes, washed and cubed*
- *4 rashes of bacon, fried until crisp*
- *2 tbs. fresh mint, chopped*
- *¼ cup whole egg mayonnaise*

Boil potatoes until tender, approx. 6-8 minutes and allow to cool completely. Mix with remaining ingredients.

# Summer Salad

**Serves 4.  A little beauty created by Rachael to get Jaxson eating salad!!**

- *4 cups mixed lettuce*
- *1 cup strawberries*
- *1 cup snow peas*
- *2 fresh mangoes, sliced*

Wash all ingredients and drain excess water.  Place lettuce into a serving bowl.  Add hulled and quartered strawberries and snow peas.  Remove skin from mango and slice flesh into the bowl.  Squeeze juice from remaining mango and lightly toss throughout the salad.  Serve and savour the flavour!

*Optional:  Substitute sliced avocado for snow peas.*


# Tomato & Bocconcini Salad

**Serves 4**

- *6 vine ripened tomatoes, sliced*
- *2 tbs. extra virgin olive oil*
- *4 bocconcini, thinly sliced*
- *½ cup fresh basil leaves*

Arrange tomato slices on a large flat serving plate, don't mind if they overlap.  Drizzle with oil and top with slices of bocconcini and basil.  Season generously with sea salt and pepper, cover and chill before serving.

*Optional:  This salad is also lovely served with the zest of a lemon grated over it.*

*Hint:  Basil leaves are best torn or used whole rather than cut with a knife as they bruise easily.  As always, the herb is best used raw as cooking diminishes its flavour.*

# Potato

You make a living by what you get
You make a life by what you give

**Unknown**

---

## Bacon Potatoes

**Makes 1.  A recipe from the lovely Katrina Price.**

- *1 large potato*
- *1 tbs. sour cream*
- *¼ tsp. French mustard*
- *2  bacon rashers, chopped and lightly cooked*

Wrap potato in alfoil and bake in 180C oven for approx. 1 hour or until cooked.  Mix together sour cream, mustard and bacon.  Scoop out 1 -2 tbs. of potato and dollop in the mixture.  Keep warm and serve as a meal or side dish.

## Chunky Skins

- *3 large potatoes, washed and peeled thickly*
- *1 tbs. extra virgin olive oil*
- *Pinch of paprika*

Brush the peels with the oil and sprinkle with paprika.  Bake 200C for 20 minutes or until crunchy and golden brown.  Serve either as a snack or with a main meal.

# Crunchy Wedges

**Serves 4. These are always a hit!**

- *2 large washed potatoes*
- *¼ cup extra virgin olive oil*
- *2 cups crushed cornflakes*
- *1 tbs. mixed herbs*

Preheat oven to 200C. Cut potatoes into wedge shapes and place in large bowl. Drizzle olive oil until all wedges are covered. Coat generously with cornflakes and herbs. Place on flat baking tray. Cook for 20 minutes and then turn and cook for a further 15 minutes.

*Optional: Can also use sweet potato. Add parmesan cheese and paprika for an extra zing. Yum!!*

# Easy Potato Bake

- *6 large potatoes, sliced thinly*
- *420g can of condensed cream of mushroom soup*
- *½ cup milk*
- *1 cup grated cheddar cheese*

Place potatoes into a casserole dish, combine soup and milk and pour over potatoes. Cover with cheese and bake in 180C oven for 45 minutes or until cooked.

# Mashed Potato

**Serves 4**

- *4 potatoes, peeled and cut*
- *2 cloves garlic, crushed*
- *1 tbs. extra virgin olive oil*

Boil and mash potatoes until nice and smooth.  Add garlic, oil and season with sea salt.


# Potato & Cheese Puffs

**Serves 4-6**

- *2-3 cups cold mashed potato*
- *2 eggs, separated*
- *½ cup grated tasty cheese*

Preheat oven to 180C.  Combine potato with egg yolks and cheese, season with sea salt and pepper.  Beat egg whites until stiff and fold into potato mixture.  Drop tbs. of mixture onto a paper lined oven tray.  Bake for 15-20 minutes until set and golden brown.

# Puffed Sweet Potato

**Serves 6**

- *2 tbs. butter*
- *2 cups mashed sweet potato*
- *½ cup milk*
- *1 egg, separated*

Melt 1 tbs. butter and to it add milk, season generously. Beat mixture into sweet potato, add yolk and mix well. Beat egg white until stiff peaks form and fold through mixture. Use 1 tbs. butter to grease a mini-muffin tray and dollop mixture into moulds, bake in a 180C oven for 20-25 minutes or until nice and golden.

# Rosemary and Thyme Roast Spuds

**Serves 6**

- *5 large scrubbed, peeled potatoes cut into thick wedges*
- *4 tbs. macadamia nut oil*
- *8 sprigs fresh rosemary*
- *8 sprigs fresh thyme*

Preheat oven to 200C. Toss spuds in oil and sprinkle with fresh herbs and some sea salt. Roast for 35-40 minutes, turning to evenly brown.

# Sliced Potato Cake

**Serves 8**

- *4-5 potatoes, peeled and thinly sliced*
- *½ cup melted butter*

Preheat oven to 200C. Cover the base of a non-stick cake tin with potato slices and sprinkle with sea salt and pepper, brush with butter. Continue layers until potatoes are used. Cover tin with alfoil and bake for 45 minutes. Remove and let stand for 5 minutes. Cut into wedges before serving.

# Sweet Potato with Orange Glaze

- *4 medium sweet potatoes*
- *½ cup orange juice*
- *2 tbs. brown sugar*
- *1 tbs. cornflour*

Cut potatoes into thick slices then dry roast in a 180C oven for 10 minutes or until just tender. In a saucepan, combine remaining ingredients with ½ cup water. Heat gently, stirring regularly until sauce has thickened. Place potato on a serving plate then cover with glaze, return to oven for 7 minutes. Garnish with orange rind.

*Hint: If you are not cooking sweet potato straight after peeling it, wrap it in alfoil to prevent it going black.*

# Scalloped Potatoes

**Serves 4**

- *4 medium potatoes peeled and sliced*
- *1 pkt French onion soup*
- *1½ cups milk*
- *2 tbs. butter, cubed*

Preheat oven to 180C. Place 1 layer of potatoes in a casserole dish and sprinkle layer with soup mix, repeat until you have used all the potatoes and soup mix. Pour over milk and top with butter cubes. Cover and cook for 1¼ hours or until potato is tender.

# Tasty Wedges

**Serves 4**

- *4 washed potatoes*
- *1 egg white, whisked*
- *1 pkt French onion or tomato soup*
- *2 tbs. macadamia nut oil*

Cut potatoes into wedges. Brush egg white, then sprinkle with your favourite soup mix. Place wedges on an oven tray and drizzle with oil. Cook in a 200C oven for 30 minutes or until crisp.

# Vegetables

It's bizarre that the produce manager
is more important to my children's health
than the pediatrician.

**Meryl Streep**

---

## Baked Spanish Onions

**Serves 6–8**

- *4 large Spanish onions, sliced*
- *4 slices multi-grain bread, grated into breadcrumbs*
- *¼ cup butter*
- *½ cup milk*

Line a pie dish with breadcrumbs, then top with a layer of sliced onions. Season with sea salt and pepper and add several bits of butter. Add another layer of crumbs repeating the layering until the dish is full. Ensure last layer is crumbs. Pour milk over contents and bake for 1½ hours in a 150C oven.

## Beans with Nutmeg

- *500g beans*
- *2 tbs. butter*
- *1 tsp. nutmeg*

Parboil beans for 1 minute then drain. Melt butter in frypan and add beans, season with nutmeg, toss over a low heat for 2-3 minutes.

# Brussel Sprout Bake

**Serves 6 and is a lovely way to eat the good old Brussel Sprout!**

- *500g brussel sprouts*
- *1 onion, chopped*
- *410g can condensed cream of celery soup*
- *¾ cup shredded cheese*

Remember when cooking with brussel sprouts to remove the tail and cut an X into the base to ensure heat penetrates the entire sprout. Cook the brussel sprouts for about 3 minutes. Drain, cool slightly and cut into quarters. Mix with remaining ingredients (reserving ¼ cup cheese) and place in a casserole dish, sprinkle remaining cheese on top. Bake for 20-30 minutes in a 180C oven.

*Optional: Brussel sprouts can be substituted with cauliflower!*

# Bubble & Squeak

- *1 cup mashed potato*
- *1 cup grated onion and shredded cabbage*
- *¼ cup extra virgin olive oil*

Mix potato, onion and cabbage, season with sea salt and pepper and form into patties. Shallow fry in hot oil until golden in colour.

*Optional: Add all other leftover vegetables (pumpkin, broccoli, corn etc) and gravy too, this moistens the mix making it 'bubble & squeak' as it cooks!*

# Cheese Topped Zucchinis

- 2 small zucchinis
- ¼ cup cheddar cheese

In a saucepan, boil zucchinis until just tender. Drain and slice in half lengthways. Sprinkle with cheddar cheese and place under a hot grill until the cheese is golden.

# Garlic Spinach

- 375g spinach
- 1 tbs. butter
- 1 clove garlic, crushed

Cook spinach in small amount of salted water for 3 minutes, then drain. Heat butter in saucepan, add garlic and fry for 1 minute. Add spinach and cook stirring for 5 minutes. Season with sea salt and pepper.

# Gingered Carrots

**Serves 4**

- 6 carrots, peeled and cut in half lengthways
- 2 tsp. fresh lemon juice
- ½ tsp. ground ginger
- 2 tbs. butter

Place carrots in a baking dish. Mix lemon juice and ginger and season with sea salt and pepper, pour over carrots then dot with butter. Cover and bake 180C for 45 minutes or until tender.

# Grilled Chilli Peaches/Nectarines

**Serves 4.  A recipe by Wendy King.**

* *8 ripe peaches or nectarines*
* *3½ tsp. sweet chilli sauce*

Preheat oven to 180C.  Cut fruit in half and remove stones.  Drizzle a small amount of chilli sauce over each piece, flesh side up.  Bake for 15 minutes to caramelise sweet chilli sauce and heat fruit through.  Can also be cooked on a BBQ.


# Herbed Zucchini

* *3 zucchinis, cut into thick diagonal slices*
* *1 tbs. butter*
* *1 tbs. finely chopped parsley*

Boil zucchinis for 3 minutes in salted water then drain well.  Heat butter in saucepan, add zucchinis and season well.  Sauté over low heat stirring occasionally until zucchinis are golden brown.  Sprinkle with chopped parsley.


# Peas with Mint & Garlic Butter

**Serves 4-6**

* *1kg pkt frozen peas*
* *20g butter, chopped*
* *1 clove garlic, crushed*
* *1/3 cup small fresh mint leaves*

Cook the peas, drain and return to dry saucepan, add butter and garlic and season with salt and pepper.  Gently toss before serving sprinkled with fresh mint leaves.

# Herb Roasted Mushrooms

**Makes 6**

- *6 large field mushrooms*
- *1 tbs. mixed herbs*
- *2 tbs. butter*

Preheat oven to 170C. degrees. Wash mushrooms and lay top side down onto a paper lined baking tray. Spread underside with butter and sprinkle with herbs. Roast for 20 minutes and serve.

# Snow Veges

**Serves 4**

- *4 cups of fresh vegetables of choice (peeled where necessary)*
- *1 pkt of white sauce mix*
- *1½ cups milk*

Steam or slow boil vegetables. Mix white sauce to manufacturer's instructions using milk and pour over vegetables and serve.

*Optional: For variation, grate some orange zest into the white sauce.*

# Spinach with Lemon

**Makes 4. This is a really nice way to each spinach!**

- *1 bunch fresh spinach, washed and shredded*
- *2 tbs. butter, softened*
- *2 tbs. lemon juice*

Place spinach in saucepan of boiling water and boil for 5 minutes or until it has wilted. Drain well and return to dry saucepan, season with sea salt and pepper. Add butter and juice and toss together.

*Optional: Another delicious way to eat spinach is to sprinkle it with mint sauce.*

# Tomatoes with Feta Cheese

**Makes 4.  A recipe by the talented Janelle McCosker.**

* *4 vine ripened tomatoes*
* *200g feta cheese*
* *1/3 cup cream*
* *12 basil leaves*

Cut top off tomatoes, scoop out flesh.  Blend cheese, cream and basil and season with pepper.  Refill tomatoes and replace lids. Place firmly in a shallow cake tin and bake in a 180C oven for 20 minutes.


# Vegetable Bake

* *500g snap frozen vegetables, thawed and drained*
* *50g edam cheese, grated*
* *1 tsp. paprika*

Place vegetables in an oven-proof dish, top with cheese and paprika.  Grill until cheese lightly browns.


# Vege Kebabs

**Makes 16.  The word 'kebab' is Arabic and means "on a skewer!" Thanks Yo Yo Tippo!**

* *1 red capsicum*
* *1 Spanish onion*
* *¼ fresh pineapple*
* *8 large mushrooms, washed and halved*

Cut first 3 ingredients into chunks and thread alternately with mushrooms onto a soaked skewer.  Grill on a hot BBQ  for a couple of minutes each side or until soft and warm.

# Zucchini Casserole

**Recipe by Gabrielle Bluett.**

- *1 tbs. extra virgin olive oil*
- *1 onion, diced*
- *3 zucchinis, sliced*
- *1 tsp. dried oregano*

Mix all ingredients together.  Place in a small casserole dish, cover and let marinate overnight in fridge.  Preheat oven to 180C and cook for 10 minutes.


# Zucchini Stir Fry

**Serves 4**

- *2 tbs. butter*
- *6 zucchinis, julienned*
- *¼ cup grated parmesan cheese*

Heat butter in frying pan and add zucchini.  Cook on medium heat for 5 minutes, stirring frequently.  Toss with sea salt and parmesan cheese just before serving.

# Mains

When in doubt ... DON'T!

**This applies to meat, men and mushrooms!!!**

## Beef

### An Aussie Steak

**Serves 2.  Recipe by Rach's Dad, Billy Moore, who has been cooking this up for as loooooong as she can remember!**

- *2 beef steaks of choice*
- *2 tsp. vegemite*
- *1½ tsb. macadamia nut oil*

Spread 1 tsp. of vegemite over each steak and let marinate for ½ an hour.  Heat the oil in a non-stick fry pan (or BBQ), add steaks and cook to your liking.

*Optional: Use some extra macadamia nut oil and cut up some potatoes into chip sized pieces and fry.*

# BBQ Beef Stir Fry

**Serves 4.  A little ripper Rachael created by accident in the middle of filming a cooking segment!!!**

- *500g lean cut beef strips*
- *2 tbs. sesame oil*
- *1 cup BBQ sauce*
- *1 capsicum, sliced thinly*

Marinate beef in BBQ sauce for 4 hours or overnight in the fridge. Heat oil in a hot wok or frying pan.  Add beef and cook on a hot temperature for 4 minutes then reduce heat.  Add sliced capsicum, cover and simmer for 5 minutes.  Serve immediately.

*Hint:  Don't cook meat as it comes straight from the refrigerator.  It is best restored to room temperature first to maximise tenderness.*

# Beef with Tangy Tomato Sauce

**Serves 4**

- *½ kg beef strips*
- *½ cup tomato paste*
- *1 large onion, chopped*
- *250g sour cream*

In a non-stick frying pan brown beef.  Add onion and simmer until cooked.  Lastly add cream and tomato paste and season to taste. Mix well, serve over rice.

*Optional:  Add a clove of crushed garlic when you add onion.*

# Beef & Potato Bake

**Serves 4.  A great way to use leftover meat and dinner is served!**

- *3 cups cubed potato*
- *2½ cups cooked, chopped roast beef*
- *300ml can of condensed tomato soup*
- *2 cups grated tasty cheese*

Combine first 3 ingredients and season.  Pour into a casserole dish, bake covered for 1 hour in a 180C oven or until potato is tender.  Sprinkle with cheese and grill until cheese has melted.

# Beef Roma Pies

**Makes 12.  Simply sensational!**

- *4 sheets puff pastry*
- *500g lean mince*
- *450g jar of your favourite pasta sauce*
- *2 cups frozen peas, corn and capsicum, thawed*

Preheat oven to 200C.  In a non-stick frying pan brown mince, add veges and season.  Pour in sauce and simmer for 10 minutes.  Whilst simmering, cut 6 large rounds into each sheet of pastry.  Line a non-stick muffin tray with first 12 rounds, spoon in mince mix and top with final rounds of pastry.  Seal with a fork.  Bake for 20 minutes or until pastry is nice and golden.

# Blue Cheese Steaks

**Serves 6**

- 6 rib eye steaks
- 200g blue vein cheese
- 2 tbs. port
- 1 tbs. butter, melted

Cut a deep pocket through the side of each steak, try to keep the opening as small as possible. Mash the cheese and mix in the port. Stuff into pockets and close with toothpicks. Season steaks with pepper and brush with butter. Cook on BBQ for about 3 minutes each side or until desired doneness.

# Carpetbag Snags

**Serves 6**

- 1kg thick beef sausages
- ½ cup BBQ sauce
- 1 tin oysters

Place sausages on a BBQ and cook over medium heat until browned. Baste with sauce towards the end of cooking. Remove from heat and allow to cool slightly, slit sausages and place 2-3 oysters in each.

# Easy Casserole

**Serves 4-6**

- *1kg round steak, cubed*
- *500g bag mixed frozen vegetables, thawed*
- *2 cups V8 juice*

Place steak and vegetables in a casserole dish, pour in V8 juice, covering contents well. Bake in 180C oven for 1½ hours or until meat is nice and tender. Serve over rice.

# Harch Steak

**Serves 2. Recipe by Karen Harch.**

- *2 steaks of choice (eye fillet, rib fillet or lamb forequarters all work well)*
- *3 tbs. tomato sauce*
- *3 tbs. bbq sauce*
- *1 tbs. Worcestershire sauce*

Preheat oven to 190C. Mix all liquid ingredients together. Place meat in a casserole dish and pour over the meat. Cover and cook for 1 hour (or until meat is cooked).

# Mustard Steak

**Serves 2. Another ripper by Tony Van Dijk – perfect for the BBQ!**

- *2 rib eye fillets*
- *2 tbs. seeded mustard*
- *2 tbs. extra virgin olive oil*
- *1 lettuce, shredded*

Marinate steaks in mustard for 2-3 hours. Pan fry steak in a little olive oil for about 4 minutes on each side. Cut steaks across the grain and serve on a bed of lettuce.


# Rach's Mustard Roast Beef

**Serves 4. This tastes absolutely incredible and is a delicious winter's evening meal!**

- *1kg prime roasting beef*
- *4 tbs. grain mustard*
- *5 tbs. macadamia nut oil*

Preheat oven to 130C. Line a baking dish with baking paper. Choose a dish just bigger than the size of the beef piece. Place beef in dish and glaze generously with mustard. Drizzle with oil and bake for 3 hours (cooking it for this time will ensure the beef is well done but still very tender). Turn beef at half way mark. Serve with your favourite roast veges and gravy.

# Roast Beef

**Serves 6-8.  *This is divine!***

- *1½ kg roast beef*
- *1 pkt French onion soup mix*
- *½ cup red wine (any you would drink)*
- *1/3 cup balsamic vinegar*

Place an upside down saucer in the bottom of your slow cooker and place roast on top of it.  Sprinkle with packet soup.  Pour wine and vinegar on top.  Cover and slow cook on low for approximately 6-7 hours (depending on your likeness) ... That's it!

*Optional:   When the roast is finished cooking,  pour the liquids into a saucepan, heat on medium and add 2 tbs. cornflour that has been stirred into a little cool water for a really flavoursome gravy!*


# Shepherd's Pie

**Serves 6.  A recipe inspired from the Gippsland Harvest Festival, Victoria.**

- *500g lean mince*
- *½ cup fruit chutney*
- *6 potatoes, boiled and mashed*
- *¾ cup grated cheese*

In a non-stick frypan brown mince, season and mix through chutney.  Pour into a casserole dish, top evenly with mashed potato and sprinkle with grated cheese.  Bake in 180C oven for 20-30 minutes or until cheese is nice and bubbly.

*Optional: Slice a tomato or two over the mince before topping with potato.*

# Silverside

**Serves 6.  A recipe from Jan Neale.**

- *1½ kg corned silverside*
- *45g pkt chicken noodle soup*
- *2 tbs. cornflour*

Place silverside and soup mix in a large saucepan, add enough water to just cover the meat.  Bring to boil, then simmer, covered, for about 2 hours or until tender.  When almost done, remove 2 cups of liquid and pour into a frying pan.  Thicken with cornflour that has been mixed into a little cool water for a flavoursome gravy.

*Optional:  Another way to flavour corned beef, is to add 1 tbs. each of vinegar and golden syrup and 6 cloves, cover and simmer.*


# Simple Beef Stroganoff

**Serves 4**

- *650g lean beef, cubed*
- *420g can condensed cream of mushroom soup*
- *115g can mushroom pieces, drained*
- *250g sour cream*

Place beef cubes in slow cooker.  Add soup and mushrooms.  Cook on low for 6 hours.  Stir in sour cream before serving and season to taste.  Alternatively, brown meat in a saucepan over low heat, add remaining ingredients and simmer until sauce thickens.

*Optional:  Delicious served over rice or penne pasta.*

# Steak Burgundy

**Serves 2.  A recipe from Paul at North Buderim Butchers**
*... Rach's favourite!*

- *2 good sized rib fillet steaks*
- *½ tbs. butter*
- *1 cup red wine*
- *1½ tsp. finely crushed garlic*

Preheat oven to 180C.  Marinate steaks in red wine for 2 hours then place each steak in an envelope of alfoil ensuring you have plenty to twist the top over to seal in steak later.  Mix butter and garlic together and place an equal dollop on top of each steak.  Seal the steak in by folding over foil.  Put on a baking tray and bake in oven for 45 minutes. YUM. YUM. YUM!

*Optional: Serve with roast vegetables or salad.*

# Steak with Mushroom Ragout

**Serves 4 and is delicious!**

- *4 steaks*
- *2 tbs. butter*
- *1 cup sliced mushrooms*
- *½ cup thickened cream*

Brush steaks with half the butter.  Preheat a frypan to hot.  Cook first sides until moisture appears (approx. 3-4 minutes), turn and cook for another 3-4 minutes for medium doneness.  Remove and cover with alfoil, allow to rest for 5 minutes.  Meanwhile, place remaining butter and mushrooms in the frypan and cook until softened.  Add cream and simmer until reduced and thickened (may need a little more cream).  Season with sea salt and pepper.

*Optional:  Serve with boiled potatoes and green beans.*

# Spicy Garlic Steak

**Serves 2.  Recipe by Paul Bermingham.**

- 1 garlic clove, finely chopped
- 1 tsp. curry powder
- ½ tsp. mixed herbs
- 2 rib fillets

Mix garlic, curry powder and mixed herbs together and coat the steak with the mixture.  Place under a grill or on the BBQ and cook to your liking.  Let steak sit for 5 minutes before slicing thinly across the grain.  Serve with salad.

# Spiced Corned Beef

**Makes 6**

- 1.5kg piece corned beef
- 1 orange, sliced
- 1/3 cup brown sugar
- 1 cinnamon stick

Place corned beef in large saucepan and just cover with water. Add the orange, brown sugar and cinnamon stick.  Bring to the boil, cover and simmer for 1½ hours or until tender. Stand for 15 minutes. *NB:* A general rule of thumb for corned beef is to allow 30 minutes per 500g.

*Optional:  Serve with a dollop of mango chutney or tomato relish and roasted veges.*

# Sweet Rissoles

**Serves 4.  Cheap, easy and delicious!**

- *340g tin of corned beef*
- *½ cup crushed pineapple, drained*
- *1 cup mashed sweet potato*
- *1 egg*

Place all ingredients into a bowl and mix thoroughly.
Roll into decent sized patties and place onto a paper lined
baking tray.  Bake in 180C oven for 30-40 minutes
or until nicely browned.

# Tasty Steak

**Serves 2.  Learnt on a trip to Rockhampton, QLD.**

- *2 pieces of blade steak*
- *1 pkt French onion soup*

Place steak on alfoil and sprinkle with enough soup to coat.  Fold
sides completely sealing the steak.  Place on a baking tray and into
a cold oven (in the centre).  Bake for 30 minutes at 130C for medium
rare and 45 minutes for medium well.

# Veal & Pesto Rolls

**Serves 4 and are *sensational*.**

- *4 veal schnitzels, flattened*
- *3 tbs. sun dried tomato pesto*
- *¼ cup grated mozzarella*
- *4 bacon rashers, rinds removed*

Combine pesto and cheese, fill schnitzels and season with sea salt and pepper. Roll firmly and wrap bacon around each. Cook in non-stick pan, turning gently until cooked through.

# Zesty Meatballs

**Makes 25**

- *500g extra lean mince*
- *½ cup tomato sauce*
- *½ cup sherry*
- *2 tbs. brown sugar*

Preheat oven to 180C. Season mince and using a tablespoon, shape into meatballs. Place meatballs on an alfoil lined baking tray and pop into oven for 30 minutes to brown. Remove and place into a casserole dish. Mix remaining ingredients and pour over meatballs. Bake for a further 30 minutes. Serve meatballs with sauce.

# Chicken

The highest reward for a person's toil
is not what they get for it,
but what they become by it!

**John Ruskin**

---

## Baked Jatz Chicken

**Serves 6**

- *6 chicken breasts*
- *½ box savoury crackers (Jatz, Ritz or similar), crushed*
- *2/3 cup natural yoghurt*

Preheat oven to 180C.  Roll chicken in yoghurt and then in cracker crumbs.  Place in a casserole dish and bake uncovered for 30 minutes, turn and bake a further 20 minutes.
Delicious served with a nice, healthy salad.

*Optional:  If breasts are large, share one between two by cutting in half.  Reduce baking time accordingly.*

# Cheese & Ham Chicken Rolls

**Serves 2**

- *2 chicken breast fillets*
- *2 pieces Swiss cheese*
- *2 pieces sliced ham*
- *1 tbs. wholegrain mustard*

Preheat oven to 180C.  Using a rolling pin, flatten chicken before smearing with mustard.  Lay a piece of cheese followed by a piece of ham on each.  Roll up and secure opening with a toothpick. Bake for 20 minutes or until brown and cooked through. Remove toothpick and cut into rounds to serve.


# Chickenloaf

**Serves 4.  Enjoyed by the whole family.**

- *500g chicken mince*
- *1 cup seasoned stuffing mix*
- *2 eggs, beaten*
- *120g tub tomato paste*

Combine chicken, stuffing mix, eggs and half the amount of tomato paste.  Shape into a log and place onto a paper lined baking tray. Spread remaining amount of tomato paste over the loaf.  Bake in 180C oven for 1 hour.

*Optional:  Grate some veges into this mix.*

*Hint:  Place bacon in the bottom of your loaf dish when making a chicken or meatloaf.  It not only adds flavour but your loaf will turn out easily without sticking.*

# Chicken Casserole

**Serves 4.  A recipe from Denise Bryant (via Kay Anderson).**

* *440g can condensed cream of chicken soup*
* *8 chicken pieces*
* *4 rashes bacon, roughly chopped*
* *4 stalks celery*

Place chicken in a casserole dish topped with bacon and celery. Add soup and bake in a 180C oven, uncovered, for 1¼ hours or until tender.

# Chicken Sausages with Pesto Mash

**Serves 4.  A recipe from Brett McCosker.**

* *8 chicken sausages*
* *4 large potatoes, cooked, drained and mashed*
* *2 tbs. basil pesto*
* *Cranberry sauce*

Add pesto to mashed potatoes.  Cook sausages in non-stick fry pan until cooked through, season to taste.  Serve sausages with a dollop of cranberry sauce and mashed potato.

# Chicken & Rice Casserole

**Serves 4**

- *4 chicken breasts*
- *1 cup rice (uncooked)*
- *1 pkt. French onion soup*
- *440g can condensed cream of celery soup*

Preheat oven to 160C. Place rice in a casserole dish with chicken on top. Combine French onion and celery soups with 2 cans of water and mix well. Pour over chicken and bake uncovered for 2 hours.

*Optional: Add some chopped onion and celery if you have.*

# Chicken with Lemon & Honey

**Serves 6. A recipe from the lovely Cathy Dineen.**

- *1 chicken, cut into pieces*
- *2 lemons, quartered*
- *2 tbs. honey*
- *2 sprigs rosemary*

Preheat oven to 180C. Put chicken skin side up in a large baking dish. Mix the juice of the lemons with the honey in a small bowl and pour over chicken pieces. Place squeezed lemon pieces in the baking dish for extra flavour. Season with sea salt and pepper. Cook for 40 minutes or until chicken is cooked and skin golden. Remove from oven and discard lemon halves. Pour juices into a saucepan and boil uncovered for about 5 mins or until the juices have thickened slightly. Serve with rice or a salad.

# Chicken Wings with Curry Honey Glaze

**Serves 6.  A recipe from Kim Morrison.**

- *2kg chicken wings*
- *¼ cup honey*
- *2 tsp. curry powder*
- *2 tsp. soy sauce*

Place chicken wings in large dish. Combine remaining ingredients in a pan, heat until honey  melts (add a little water if too thick). Pour over chicken wings.  Marinate for several hours or refrigerate overnight.  BBQ wings until cooked through.  Baste frequently during cooking process.

# Cranberry & Orange Chicken

**Serves 4.  Y.u.m.m.y!**

- *4 chicken breasts*
- *1 pkt. French onion soup*
- *¾ cup cranberry sauce*
- *¾ cup orange juice*

Place chicken breasts in casserole dish.  Mix soup, cranberry sauce, and orange juice in a medium bowl and pour over chicken. Cover and cook in a 150C oven for 1 hour.

# Curry Mayonnaise Chicken

**Serves 2-3**

- *6 chicken legs*
- *1/3 cup mayonnaise*
- *3 tsp. curry powder*
- *2 slices wholemeal bread, grated into breadcrumbs*

Combine mayonnaise and curry, coat legs with the mixture. Roll in breadcrumbs and bake in a 180C oven for 45 minutes or until tender.

# Feta Chicken

**Serves 2**

- *2 chicken breasts*
- *250g feta cheese with basil and tomato*
- *3 tbs. macadamia nut oil*
- *½ cup breadcrumbs*

Gently mallet chicken to thin slightly. Place 2 very generous strips of feta in the middle of a chicken breast and fold over, secure with a toothpick or two. Coat with oil and roll in breadcrumbs. Bake in 180C oven for 20 minutes or until meat is cooked.

*Optional: Use seasoned stuffing mix instead of breadcrumbs.*

# Curried, Honey Mustard Chicken

**Serves 4.  Recipe by Cameron Hewitt.  Quick, easy and ultra delicious!**

- *4 chicken breasts*
- *1/3 cup honey*
- *1/3 cup curry powder*
- *1/3 cup seeded mustard*

Preheat oven to 180C.  Cut the chicken into large fillets.  Mix honey, curry powder and mustard together.   Coat the chicken with the mixture and place on paper lined baking tray.  Bake for 25 minutes or until done.

# Magic Mango Chicken

**Serves 4.  Rachael created this little beauty by accident – little fat and tastes brilliant!!!!!!!**

- *2 chicken breasts, sliced into strips*
- *3 tbs. macadamia nut oil*
- *1 chicken stock cube in 1 cup of boiling water*
- *1 fresh mango, peeled and sliced*

Heat oil in a wok or frying pan.  Add chicken and fry till golden brown.  Reduce heat and add stock and the mango slices.  Simmer for around 15 minutes and serve.

*Optional:  Serve with rice and a few of your favourite veges.*

# Olive Chicken Patties

**Serves 4**

- *1 large egg*
- *1 cup seasoned croutons*
- *1/3 cup black olive tapenade*
- *½ kg chicken mince*

Mix all ingredients together. Shape into patties, place on a non-stick baking tray under a medium grill. Grill in oven, turning until fully cooked (approx. 15-20 minutes).

*Optional: Serve on a roll with fresh salad.*

# Orange Roast Chicken

**Serves 4. Recipe by Carly Nelson, a beauty for Sunday roasts or even on the table at Christmas time!**

- *1 large uncooked chicken*
- *2 oranges*
- *1 tbs. fresh mixed herbs*
- *½ cup macadamia nut oil*

Preheat oven to 180C. Place chicken in a baking paper lined roasting tray breast side up. Drizzle with oil. Grate the skin of one of the oranges and juice both oranges over the chicken. Finally sprinkle herbs over the top and roast chicken for 1½ hours or until cooked to your liking. Remove from oven and cover with alfoil, allow to rest for 5 minutes before cutting and serving.

*Hint: It usually takes 30 minutes per 500g of weight to cook a chicken in a preheated oven at 180C.*

# Roma Chicken

**Serves 4. A recipe from Katrina Price.**

- ½ cooked chicken, remove skin
- 375ml bottle of your favourite tomato based pasta sauce
- 2 tbs. sour cream
- 1 capsicum, de-seeded and sliced

Cut up chicken, mix with pasta sauce and capsicum in a saucepan. Season to taste. Bring to the boil stirring in sour cream at the end. Reduce heat and simmer for 5 minutes.

# Swiss Schnitzel

**Serves 4. A fabulous recipe from the lovely Lynette Willson.**

- 2 chicken breasts
- 3 slices of multigrain bread, grated into crumbs
- 2 tbs. extra virgin olive oil
- 4 slices Jarlsberg cheese

Cut chicken in half, then using a rolling pin or mallet pound slices until thin. Coat with breadcrumbs, pressing into flesh to coat both sides. Heat oil in a large non-stick frying pan. Over moderate heat cook schnitzels 2 at a time for 2 minutes, until golden on the bottom, turn and top with cheese. Cook for a further 3 minutes or until chicken is tender and the cheese melts.

# Tangy Chicken Tenderloins

**Serves 4**

- *3 chicken breasts, sliced*
- *3 tbs. flour*
- *1 cup bbq sauce*
- *½ cup orange juice*

Coat chicken with flour. Brown in a non-stick pan and place in a shallow baking pan. Mix bbq sauce and orange juice and pour over chicken. Bake covered in a 180C oven for 15 minutes. Remove from oven, spoon sauce over chicken and bake uncovered for another 10-15 minutes.

# Yummy Drummies

**Serves 4**

- *2 tbs. lemon juice*
- *4 tbs. honey*
- *2 tbs. soy sauce*
- *8 chicken drumsticks, skinned*

Blend honey, soy sauce and lemon juice together to make a marinade. Place chicken in a casserole dish and pour marinade over the top of each piece. Cover and refrigerate for 2 hours. Preheat oven to 220C and cook chicken for around 40-50 minutes or until cooked throughout. Serve with vegetable of choice.

# Fish

Life is a journey that is homeward bound.

**Anonymous**

---

## Almond Fish Fillets

**Serves 4. Paul Bermingham's little beauty that the kids just love.**

- *8 pieces white fish fillets*
- *1 cup plain flour*
- *1½ cups crushed almonds*
- *1 cup organic mayonnaise*

Preheat oven to 180C. Coat fillets with mayonnaise. Combine plain flour and almonds mixing well and roll fillets in dry ingredients. Place on a lined baking tray and bake for 15-20 minutes.

*Optional: Serve with summer salad when it's hot or with yummy green veges in winter. You can also substitute this with chicken and it works beautifully – you just need to cook for 10 minutes longer.*

# Apricot Fish

**Serves 4. Yummy!**

- *500g fresh white fish fillets*
- *3 tbs. fresh lemon juice*
- *1/3 cup natural yoghurt*
- *3 tbs. apricot jam*

Place lemon juice in a baking dish with fish. Bake at 180C uncovered for 5 minutes then drain. Meanwhile, combine remaining ingredients and spoon over fish. Return to oven for 3 minutes or until cooked.

# Baked Fish

**Serves 2**

- *2 fresh white fish fillets*
- *1 tsp. butter*
- *1 lemon*

Coat fish with melted butter and season with sea salt and pepper. Cut lemon and place slices on fish. Wrap fish in alfoil. Cook in 180C oven for 20 minutes or until fish is tender.

*Optional: Can sprinkle a little garlic or herbs on fish before wrapping.*

# Cheesy Fish Steaks

**Serves 4**

- *4 fish steaks, swordfish or mahi mahi etc*
- *¾ cup grated cheese*
- *1 tsp. Worcestershire sauce*
- *1 tbs. milk*

Place fish steaks under a 160C grill for 5 minutes. Mix remaining ingredients and season with sea salt and pepper. Turn the fish and spread the uncooked side with cheese mix. Grill for a further 5 minutes or until fish is cooked and the topping bubbling.

*Optional: Garnish with fresh chopped parsley, also nice made with salmon steaks.*

# Dukkah Crusted Salmon

**Serves 4 and is *absolutely* delish ...**

- *4 skinless salmon fillets*
- *Macadamia nut oil spray*
- *1/3 cup dukkah*

Place salmon on an alfoil lined baking tray. Lightly spray each fillet with oil, then press dukkah onto both sides of each fillet.
Bake at 150C for 15 minutes or to your liking.

# Easy Salmon Rissoles

**Serves 4. A recipe from Marie McColl ... Quick, easy & delicious!**

- *415g tin pink salmon*
- *½ cup whole-egg mayonnaise*
- *1 cup mashed potato*
- *1 cup crushed Jatz cracked black pepper bickies*

Mix all ingredients together and season with pepper. Shape into cakes and bake in a 180C oven for 20 minutes or until golden.

# Lemon Fish

**Serves 4**

- *4 fish fillets*
- *1 lemon, juiced*
- *1 tbs. butter*
- *2 tbs. freshly chopped parsley*

Season fish with pepper. Place under grill. Mix butter, juice and ½ tsp. rind together and spread over fish. Grill until lightly browned. Turn carefully then spread with remaining lemon mix. Grill until cooked. Serve garnished with lemon slices and parsley.

*Hint: Often a nice accompaniment to fish is a glass of water with ice cubes that have been frozen with little slices of lemon in them.*

# Lime & Salmon Cakes

**Serves 6. Y.u.m.m.y!**

- *1 lime*
- *415g can pink salmon, drained*
- *1 egg*
- *3 slices wholemeal bread, grated into crumbs*

Grate lime zest, then juice the lime. Place zest, juice and remaining ingredients in a bowl, season with pepper. Mix well before shaping into 12 thick cakes. Cook in a greased non-stick pan until heated through.

*Hint: Fresh bread is easier to grate when frozen.*


# Salmon Delight

**Serves 4. A recipe from the vibrant Katrina Price.**

- *4 salmon steaks, skinless*
- *4 slices prosciutto*
- *200g green beans, top 'n' tailed*
- *12 cherry tomatoes*

Wrap the salmon steaks in prosciutto and place in a baking dish. Add the cherry tomatoes and beans. Preheat oven to 180C and bake for 10-15 minutes.

*Optional: For a special occasion top with some toasted pinenuts and a drizzle of lemon juice.*

# Salmon Mornay

**Serves 4**

- *415g can pink salmon*
- *2 tsp. lemon juice*
- *440g can condensed cream of celery soup*
- *½ cup grated cheese*

Combine salmon, juice and soup, season with cracked pepper. Place in an oven proof dish, top with cheese and bake at 190C for 30 minutes.

*Optional: Add some chopped onion or celery if you have.*


# Salmon Wellington

**Serves 4. A recipe from the lovely Wendy Beattie, great for a dinner party!**

- *4 salmon steaks, skin off*
- *2 sheets puff pastry*
- *8 cherry tomatoes*
- *2 tbs. basil pesto*

Cut puff pastry sheets in half and smooth ½ tbs. of pesto down the middle of each half. Place Salmon on top of pesto and slice cherry tomatoes on top of salmon. Season with sea salt and pepper if you like. Roll pastry over salmon ensuring all edges are sealed. Cook in preheated 180C oven for 30 minutes or until golden brown.

*Optional: Before sealing, drizzle with freshly squeezed lemon juice. For added effect, sprinkle sesame seeds on top before baking.*

# Salsa Surprise Fish

**Serves 4.  This will surprise and delight!**

- *500g fresh white fish fillets*
- *½ cup thick and chunky salsa*
- *2 tbs. honey*
- *2 tbs. Dijon mustard*

Place fish in a paper lined baking dish.  Bake at 180C uncovered for 5 minutes then drain.  Meanwhile, combine remaining ingredients and pour over fish.  Return to oven for 3 minutes or until sauce is heated.

# Swiss Fish

**Serves 4**

- *4 fillets of sea perch, dory or large whiting*
- *1 ripe avocado*
- *2 tbs. butter*
- *4 slices Swiss cheese*

Preheat oven to 180C.  Melt butter in a non-stick frypan on medium heat.  Add fish fillets, cooking on 1 side for approx. 2 minutes before flipping (cooking time is dependant on how thick the fish fillet is). Lay cooked fillets on a tray lined with baking paper and top with Swiss cheese.  Melt in oven for about 5 minutes and then top with a sliver or two of avocado and serve with salad.

# Tarragon Fish

**Serves 4**

- *500g fresh white fish fillets*
- *½ cup natural yoghurt*
- *1 tsp. dried tarragon*
- *2 tbs. grated tasty cheese*

Place fish in a greased baking dish. Bake in a 180C oven uncovered for 5 minutes, then drain. Meanwhile, combine remaining ingredients and spread over fish. Return to oven for 3 minutes or until cheese has melted.


# Tuna & Tomato Risotto

**Serves 4. A recipe from the talented Marie McColl.**

- *425g can flaked tuna in brine, drained*
- *410g can chopped tomatoes*
- *2 cups arborio rice*
- *5 cups seafood or vegetable stock*

Bring stock to boil, add rice and reduce heat and simmer for 20 minutes. Add tuna and tomatoes, season to taste. Continue to simmer, stirring regularly, until all liquid has absorbed. Then serve.

# Lamb

Laughter is brightest where food is best.

**Irish Proverb**

---

## Asian BBQ Lamb Chops

**Serves 4**

- *8 lamb chops*
- *3 tsp. soy sauce*
- *3 tbs. sweet chilli sauce*

Mix soy and sweet chilli sauces. Cook chops on BBQ for 1-2 minutes each side. Reduce heat and continue cooking for 2-3 minutes while brushing with baste. Cover loosely with alfoil and allow to rest for 5 minutes before serving.

## Balsamic Glazed Lamb Cutlets

**Serves 4 and is an absolute *WINNER!***

- *12 lamb cutlets*
- *1 tbs. balsamic vinegar*
- *1 tbs. honey*
- *2 tbs. fresh rosemary leaves*

Heat frypan, grill or BBQ. Mix last 3 ingredients. Cook cutlets for 1-2 minutes each side or until just starting to brown. Brush with baste and cook a further 3 minutes each side, basting occasionally. Serve drizzled with the tasty jus.

---

# Chilli Lamb Rissoles

**Makes 8**

- *500g lamb mince*
- *1 egg, lightly beaten*
- *1 cup rolled oats*
- *¼ cup sweet chilli sauce*

Combine all ingredients together in a bowl and season with sea salt and pepper.  Form into rissoles, heat a non-stick pan or greased BBQ plate, and cook turning occasionally for 15 minutes or until cooked through depending on size.


# Chinese-Style Lamb Roast

**Serves 4-6.  Try it ... You'll be surprised!**

- *1.5kg lamb roast*
- *375ml can evaporated milk*
- *½ cup hoisin or teriyaki sauce*

Place the lamb into an oven bag.  Combine the milk and sauce.  Pour about half over the lamb (remaining can be frozen for another time) and tightly seal the bag, piercing a few holes around the end.  Roast the lamb in a 180C oven for 1 hour and 45 minutes or until desired doneness.  Serve with fried rice.

*Optional:  Garnish with fresh coriander.*

# Curry Lamb Pies

**Makes 8.  Great in winter!**

- *4 slices of wholemeal bread, remove crusts and flatten slightly*
- *1 tbs. butter*
- *400g can lamb curry*

Butter bread both sides.  Using a scone cutter, cut rounds from bread and press into patty cake pan.  Bake in 180C oven for 5 minutes or until golden brown.  Heat lamb curry and spoon into cases.

# Glazed Lamb Chops

**Serves 4-6**

- *4 to 6 lamb loin chops, about 2cm thick*
- *1/3 cup orange marmalade*
- *2 tbs. lemon juice*

Place lamb under a grill for 6 minutes, season and turn.
Grill the other side for 5 minutes, or until almost cooked to desired doneness.  Season second side.  Combine the marmalade and lemon juice, spread evenly over the lamb chops and grill for about 2 minutes longer.

# Irish Stew

**Serves 4-6**

- *1kg lamb neck chops*
- *3 large onions, sliced*
- *1 kg potatoes, sliced*
- *2 tbs. Worcestershire sauce*

Arrange a layer of chops in a flame proof casserole dish. Season with sea salt and pepper. Cover with a layer of onions and then potatoes. Repeat until all used. Sprinkle sauce over the top, then pour in enough water to come two-thirds up the dish. Place on cook top and bring to the boil, cover, and transfer to a preheated 160C oven for 2½ hours.

*Optional: Can use beef stock instead of water. Add whatever veges you have in the fridge.*

# Lamb & Pea Stroganoff

**Serves 4**

- *1 tbs. butter*
- *500g lamb, diced*
- *1½ cups frozen peas*
- *½ cup cream*

Heat a frying pan on high, add butter and when melted add lamb. Brown quickly tossing the meat frequently. Add the peas, cream and season to taste. Reduce the heat to low and cover the pan, simmer for 10 minutes or until the peas are tender.

# Lamb Rissoles

**Makes 8. Y.U.M.M.Y!!!**

- *500g lamb mince*
- *1 onion grated*
- *2 tbs. mint jelly*

Preheat oven 180C.  Combine all ingredients and season with sea salt and pepper.  Form into rissoles and bake in moderate oven for 20 minutes or until cooked through.

*Optional:   These are also fine to pan-fry and are delicious served with a dollop of Raita.*


# Lamb Samosas

**Makes 12**

- *2 tbs. butter*
- *500g lamb mince*
- *½ a 283g can Tikka Masala (medium)*
  *– remainder can be frozen for later*
- *12 filo pastry sheets*

Fry mince in a non-stick frying pan with a little butter until brown. Add curry and cook a further 2 minutes then set aside.  Preheat oven to 190C.  Melt remaining butter, cut pastry sheets in half lengthways.  Brush one strip of pastry with butter, then lay another strip on top and brush again.  Place a generous spoonful of lamb in the corner of the strip and fold over to form a triangular package, continue to fold.  Brush with butter and place on a baking sheet. Repeat using the remaining ingredients.  Bake for 15-20 minutes until golden.  Serve hot.

*Optional:   These are DELICIOUS served with sweet chilli sauce and are a real hit made smaller as a nibble when friends and family gather!*

# Moroccan Spiced Lamb

**Serves 2.  A recipe from the lovely Lisa Darr.**

- *2 lamb backstraps*
- *1 tbs. macadamia nut oil*
- *2 tsp. Moroccan spice*

Preheat oven to 220C.  Rub flesh of lamb with oil, then coat well with the spice.  Place on a baking tray and roast for 15 minutes for medium or until cooked to your liking.  Remove lamb, cover with alfoil and allow to rest for 10 minutes before serving.

*Optional:  According to Chef, Peter Wolf from the Eumundi Markets ... To cook on a BBQ simply heat grill to hot and for well done cook 4 minutes each side, for medium 3 minutes, and rare 2 minutes.*

# Pesto Lamb

**Serves 2.  A great little creation of Rachael's inspired by her local butcher!**

- *4 lamb cutlets*
- *2tbs. basil pesto*
- *1 tsp. finely grated lemon rind*
- *3 tbs. butter*

Preheat oven to 180C. Combine basil pesto, lemon rind and butter. Place each cutlet in an envelope of alfoil and dollop a tbs. of mixture on top of all the cutlets.  Fold the alfoil to seal firmly and cook for 30 minutes.

*Optional:  Substitute basil pesto and lemon rind with 4 tbs. garlic flavoured pasta sauce and some parmesan cheese.*

# Prosciutto & Pesto Cutlets

**Serves 4.  A beauty from Brian Neale, Byron Bay NSW.**

- *4 slices prosciutto*
- *8 lamb cutlets*
- *¼ cup basil pesto*

Spread cutlets with pesto.  Wrap with prosciutto.  Grill each side until cutlets are cooked.  Simply delicious served with a salad.

# Roast Lamb

- *1½ kg leg of lamb*
- *2 tbs. extra virgin olive oil*
- *2tbs. honey*
- *1 tbs. wholegrain mustard*

Preheat oven to 180C.  Use a knife to make small cuts in the meat, rub with oil.  Mix mustard and honey together and baste the meat, rubbing the mixture into the cuts.  Bake for 1½ hours for rare to medium or 2 hours for medium to well done.

*Optional:  Press fresh rosemary twigs into the cuts.*

*Hint #1:  With any roast lamb, the flavour can be enhanced by making tiny slits in the meat and filling them with fresh mint before roasting. Or simply baste with yoghurt or orange juice during cooking.*

*Hint #2:  When cooking a roast, instead of oil place water in the baking pan.*

# Pasta

Minds are like parachutes, they only function when open.

**Thomas Dewar**

---

## Chorizo Gnocchi

**Serves 4**

- *1 small red onion, diced*
- *2 chorizo sausages, thinly sliced*
- *1 pkt. Fresh potato gnocchi, cooked and drained*
- *575g jar Napolitano pasta sauce*

Cook onion and chorizo together in a large non-stick pan for 3 minutes or until golden.  Add gnocchi , sauce and ¼ cup water.  Season with sea salt and pepper.  Simmer for 20 minutes or until heated through.

*Optional:  Top with freshly grated parmesan to serve.*


## Creamy Pasta Sauce

**Serves 4.  A recipe from Jan Neale.**

- *4 shallots, finely chopped*
- *4 rashers bacon, chopped*
- *200g button mushrooms, sliced*
- *200g tub cream cheese, softened*

Combine shallots and bacon in large fying pan, stir until bacon is crisp.  Add mushrooms, stir until softened.  Add cream cheese and a third cup of boiling water, simmer until cheese is melted.

# Creamy Pesto Chicken Gnocchi

**Serves 4**

- *300ml cream*
- *¼ cup basil pesto*
- *2 cups coarsely chopped, cooked chicken*
- *500g gnocchi*

Simmer cream and pesto in a frying pan for 5 minutes.
Add chicken and gnocchi, mix well and serve warm.

*Optional: Sprinkle with basil leaves or parmesan cheese.*


# Easy Macaroni Cheese

**Serves 4. A recipe by Michelle Dodd.**

- *400g macaroni*
- *1/3 cup pouring cream*
- *1¼ cups milk*
- *1½ cups grated cheddar cheese*

Cook the macaroni in a large saucepan of boiling water for
6 minutes or until al dente. Drain and return to the saucepan.
Add the cream, milk and cheese to the pan, stir over a low heat until
the cheese melts and the mixture is thick and coats the pasta.

# Fettuccine Alfredo

**Serves 4**

- ¼ cup butter
- 1 cup heavy cream
- 1 cup freshly grated Parmesan
- 350g fresh fettuccine

While boiling pasta, melt butter in a large fry pan and add cream bringing it to the boil.  Simmer for 5 minutes, stirring constantly, add ¾ of the Parmesan cheese and season well.  Reduce heat, add drained (not rinsed) pasta and toss until thoroughly coated.  Serve sprinkled with remaining Parmesan.

# Fettuccine Chicken

**Serves 4.  A tasty pasta dish from Nikki Goodwin.**

- 1 cup cooked chicken
- 500g pkt fettuccine pasta
- 420g can cream of condensed chicken soup

Cook Fettuccine to manufacturer's instructions.  Drain excess water and add chicken and soup, stir to heat throughout and serve.

*Optional:  Sprinkle with some grated cheese or add some quartered snow peas or vegetable of choice.*

# Macaroni Bake

**Serves 4.  A recipe from the wonderful Jenny Postle.**

- *2 cups cooked macaroni*
- *420g can tomato soup*
- *250g diced ham or bacon*
- *1 cup grated Colby cheese*

Place macaroni, soup and ham in a bowl and mix well before pouring into a casserole dish.  Top with grated cheese and bake in a 180C oven for 20 minutes.

*Optional:  Mix some freshly grated breadcrumbs into the cheese topping.*

# Mary's Spaghetti Sauce

**Serves 2**

- *1 onion, sliced finely*
- *2 bacon rashers, sliced finely*
- *400g lean mince*
- *420g can of condensed tomato soup*

In a fry pan sauté onion.  Add bacon and cook until brown. Add mince and cook to your liking.  Add enough soup to create a thickened consistency and serve.

*Optional:  This is a stand-alone recipe or you can serve it with your favourite pasta or on some toast.  Quick and easy and very tasty.*

# Pasta & Broccoli

**Serves 4. A southern Calabrese Italian recipe from Peter Paladino.**

- *500g pkt spaghetti pasta*
- *1/3 cup extra virgin olive oil*
- *2 cloves garlic, crushed*
- *3 heads of broccoli*

Bring 3 ltr. of salted water to the boil. Add broccoli and simmer. When half cooked, add pasta, cooking according to packet instructions. Strain pasta and broccoli into a colander.
In the cooking pot, heat the oil and garlic over a medium heat for 1-2 minutes. Return pasta and broccoli to the pot stirring to combine. *NB*: The broccoli should be well broken down and little bits stuck to each strand of pasta.

*Optional: Serve with grated parmesan if you like.*


# Pesto Pasta

**Serves 4**

- *450g pkt linguine pasta*
- *340g basil pesto*
- *2 cups grape or cherry tomatoes, cut in half*
- *1½ cup grated parmesan cheese*

Cook pasta as per instructions. Stir in basil pesto, tossing gently over low heat until pasta is coated. Add grape tomatoes and toss for 1 minute. Sprinkle with cheese and serve.

*Optional: Roast seasoned tomatoes in a 180C oven for 5 minutes first.*

# Pinenut Pasta

**Serves 2.  Recipe by forever NSW loyal Lea 'Boof' Van Dijk.**

- *½ pkt spinach fettucine*
- *¾ cup pinenuts*
- *1 tbs. butter*
- *½ cup grated parmesan cheese*

Put butter and pinenuts in a warm fry pan and cook until golden brown.  Bring a saucepan of water to the boil and cook pasta to packet instructions.   Drain water and toss pasta with pineuts and parmesan.

*Optional:  A little cracked pepper tastes great too.*


# Prosciutto Pasta

**Serves 2**

- *3 slices prosciutto*
- *½ pkt of thin spaghetti*
- *1½ tbs. extra virgin olive oil*
- *1½ cup grated parmesan cheese*

Bring a saucepan of water to the boil and cook pasta to packet instructions. Thinly slice prosciutto and mix with parmesan cheese. Drain pasta and add the oil. Stir in prosciutto and cheese and serve.

*Optional:  Top with a little parsley.*

# Pork

As a child my family's menu consisted of two choices:
Take it or leave it!

**Buddy Hackett**

---

## A Pie for A Guy

**Serves 4. A recipe from Shane Hunia, Corramandel N.Z.**

- *2 sheets puff pastry, thawed*
- *½ an onion, diced*
- *4 rashers of bacon, roughly chopped*
- *6 eggs*

Place first sheet of puff pastry in a medium sized greased or paper lined quiche dish. Cover the base with onion and then bacon. Crack each egg (without breaking the yolk) spanning the entire base. Season generously with sea salt and pepper before topping with final sheet of pastry. Using a fork, seal the edges and trim excess pastry. Pierce the lid 4 times and bake in a 200C oven for 25 minutes.

# Bacon & Cannellini Risotto

**Serves 4 and is S.c.r.u.m.p.t.i.o.u.s!**

- *4 rashers of bacon, roughly chopped*
- *5 cups chicken stock*
- *2 cups arborio rice*
- *400g can cannellini beans*

Whilst frying bacon in a large non-stick frying pan, bring stock to boil in a saucepan. Add rice to frying pan with bacon and stir to coat, add stock, reduce heat, cover and simmer for 20 minutes.
Add beans, season with sea salt and pepper. Continue to simmer until rice is soft and stock has been fully absorbed.

*Optional: Replace cannellini beans with peas.*


# Easy Pork Bites

**Makes 36. A recipe from the brilliant Michelle Dodd ...**
***Soooooooo easy!***

- *6 flavoured sausages eg.,*
  *Italian, herb and garlic, honey and rosemary,*
  *rosemary and lamb ... Whatever takes your fancy!*

Squeeze the contents of sausages into a bowl. Roll into bite-sized balls, place on an alfoil lined baking tray and bake in a 180C oven for 10 minutes or until cooked. Serve warm with your favourite sauce.

# Country BBQ Pork Ribs

**Serves 4**

- *1kg pork ribs*
- *2 large onions, sliced*
- *1 clove garlic, minced*
- *1 bottle of your favourite bbq sauce*

Place ribs in bottom of slow cooker. Add onions, garlic, and sauce. Cover and cook on low for 7-8 hours.


# Ham on the Bone

**Serves 8.  A recipe by the *funky* Franj Oberman.**

- *½ cup brown sugar*
- *1 cup apricot jam*
- *1½ kg leg of ham*
- *¼ cup cloves*

Place brown sugar and jam in a saucepan and dissolve. Remove outer skin of ham and score creatively with a sharp knife. Place cloves in scored corners then glaze. Place ham in 150C oven for an hour or until "you like what you see." Carve and serve.

*Glaze Options:*

- *2 cups brown sugar, ½ cup honey, juice from one can of pineapple rings. Mix until smooth and spoon half over the ham, applying remainder half way through baking*
- *Cloves and honey*
- *English mustard and demerara sugar*
- *3 pineapple rings, half of a can of pineapple juice, and 1 tbs. honey. Put all ingredients into a blender ... Then cook in a small saucepan until desired thickness*

# Glazed Pork Tenderloins

**Serves 4. A recipe from the bright and bubbly
Julie McDonald OAM.**

- *2 pork tenderloins (approx. 500g)*
- *1/3 cup salt reduced soy sauce*
- *2 tbs. honey*
- *2 tbs. Worcestershire sauce*

Trim the tenderloins of excess fat.  Combine the soy, honey and
Worcestershire sauce in a shallow dish with the tenderloins.
Cover and refrigerate overnight, turning several times.
Grill the pork over a medium grill for about 20 minutes or
to prepare in the oven, bake at 160C for about 50 minutes,
basting periodically.

# Pork & Asparagus Casserole

**Serves 4**

- *440g condensed cream of asparagus soup*
- *2 granny smith apples*
- *4 pork chops, trimmed of fat*

Peel and slice apples.  Put can of soup, apple and pork in saucepan.
Simmer until pork is tender (approx. 1 hour).

*Optional:  Add some sultanas and serve with your favourite roast
veges.*

# Pork Fillets with Dried Fruit

**Serves 2.  These are** *d.e.l.i.c.i.o.u.s!*

- 2 pork fillets
- 1 cup dried fruit
- ½ onion, finely chopped
- 2 rashers bacon

Soak fruit in boiling water for 10 minutes or until plump and soft, then drain.  Cut a lengthways slit ¾ way through each fillet.  Fry onion until brown and mix with fruit.  Press into each fillet, wrap in bacon and tie with string.  Seal all over in hot pan, then bake in 180C oven for 20 minutes.


# Pork & Pumpkin Curry

**Serves 4**

- ½ kg pork, cubed
- ½ kg pumpkin, cubed
- 2 tbs. red curry paste
- 410g tin coconut cream

Over medium heat, brown pork in a large saucepan, add curry paste and stir, cooking for 5 minutes.  Pour cream into pan, add ½ cup water and pumpkin, season to taste and bring to the boil.  Reduce heat and simmer for 30-40 minutes or until the pork is cooked.

*Optional:  This is best made a few hours prior to serving as it thickens as it cools.  Simply reheat when ready to serve.*

# Pork Roll

**Serves 4**

- *500g pork sausages*
- *1 cup fresh breadcrumbs*
- *1 egg*
- *1 onion, grated*

Cut away skin from sausages. Mix pork, egg and onion together and season with sea salt and pepper. Form into a loaf and roll in breadcrumbs. Place in a baking dish and bake in a pre-heated 180C oven turning after 20 minutes. Then cook for a further 20 minutes.

*Optional: Serve bathed in apple sauce ... Surprisingly yummy!*


# Sausage Snacks

**Serves 4. A recipe from Errol McCosker.**

- *4 large pork sausages*
- *4 tbs. sweet mustard pickle*
- *2 cups mashed potato*
- *2 tbs. finely chopped chives or parsley (optional)*

Grill or fry sausages, cool slightly then split open lengthways. Spread with pickle. Mix chives through mashed potato and spoon onto sausages, place under grill and cook until golden brown.

*Optional: Sweet mustard pickle can be substituted with tomato sauce.*

# Sausages in Apples

**Makes 4**

- *4 sausages*
- *4 large granny smith apples, cored*

Pierce sausages several times then press into centre of apples. Score the apple skin, place on a lined baking tray and bake in a 180C oven for 1 hour.


# Tasty Ham Dinner

**Serves 6.  A recipe from Shane McCosker ... Great for the whole family!**

- *180g pkt Rice-A-Riso*
- *1½ cups cubed, cooked ham*
- *1 cup frozen peas, thawed*
- *1½ cups grated cheddar cheese*

Prepare rice as per instructions.  In a large bowl, combine rice, ham, peas and 1 cup of cheese.  Season with sea salt and pepper.  Pour into baking dish and top with remaining cheese and bake in 180C oven for 20 minutes.

# Vegetarian Mains

Success usually comes to those
who are too busy to be looking for it.

**Henry David Thoreau**

## Asparagus and Egg Patties

**Makes 4**

- *6 eggs, hard boiled and chopped*
- *½ cup tinned asparagus cuts*
- *1 cup cooked mashed potato*
- *1 cup cooked rice*

Combine all ingredients and season with sea salt and pepper.
Form into patties, place on a lined baking tray and bake in a
preheated 180C oven for 20 minutes or until golden brown.

*Optional: Asparagus can be substituted with a 125g tin of corn
kernels. Delicious served with a salad and dollop of aioli.*

# Baked Rice Pilaf

**Serves 4. A second generation recipe from the beautiful
Fleur Welligan.**

- *1 onion, peeled and diced*
- *2 cloves garlic, chopped*
- *1 cup basmati rice*
- *2 cups chicken stock*

Sauté onion in a little water. Add garlic and rice and stir. Add stock
and bring to the boil. Transfer mixture to a baking dish, cover and
bake at 180C for 30 minutes. Remove from oven and fluff rice with a
fork.

*Optional: Stir through a knob of butter and some chopped parsley if
desired.*


# Baked Ricotta Pie

**Serves 6-8 ... This is *super yummy* served with a salad
and delicious dressing!**

- *1 kg fresh ricotta*
- *3 eggs, lightly beaten*
- *3 tbs. fresh thyme leaves*
- *Macadamia nut oil spray*

Preheat oven 200C. Spray a 22cm round spring form cake tin with
oil. Place ricotta and eggs in a bowl and stir to combine. Using
a spatula, pour mixture into tin, sprinkle generously with thyme
and season with pepper. Bake for 35-40 minutes or until firm and
golden. Allow to cool before removing from tin.

*Optional: These can also be made in muffin trays, reduce baking time
to 15 minutes or until the pies are firm and golden.*

# Bean Baskets

**Makes 4**

- *4 flour tortillas*
- *420g can mean beanz Mexican jackel, heated*
- *1 cup coarsely grated cheese*
- *¼ cup sour cream*

Mould tortillas into muffin pans and bake in 150C oven for 5-6 minutes or until golden. Divide beans among baskets. Top with a dollop of sour cream and grated cheese.


# Buttered Couscous

**Serves 4**

- *2½ cups chicken stock*
- *2½ cups couscous*
- *3 tbs. butter*

Heat chicken stock in a saucepan, add couscous and butter. Mix well and allow to stand for 5 minutes before serving.

*Couscous Options:*

- *Roasted pumpkin dusted in Moroccan Spice, finely diced red onion, toasted pinenuts*
- *Fresh parsley, mint, lemon juice and zest*
- *Tuna, finely diced red onion and coriander*
- *Toasted pinenuts, sultanas and fresh mint*
- *Capsicum, slivered almonds, sultanas and baby spinach*

# Cheddar & Basil Tortillas

**Serves 1**

- *1 tbs. butter*
- *2 soft flour tortillas*
- *1/3 cup grated cheddar cheese*
- *¼ cup fresh basil leaves*

Heat butter in a non-stick frying pan over medium heat. Add one tortilla, layer with cheese then basil and season with sea salt and pepper, cook for 2 minutes or until underneath is golden brown. Top with remaining tortilla and flip. Cook for a further 2-3 minutes. Slide from pan onto a chopping board and cut into wedges. Serve immediately with a salad.

*Optional: Substitute basil with semi-dried tomatoes, mushrooms, relish or whatever you like.*

# Cheesy Pasta Bake

**Serves 4. A recipe by Marie McColl.**

- *3 cups spiral noodles, cooked*
- *1 pkt chicken and leek soup (or your favourite soup)*
- *¾ cup grated tasty cheese*
- *2½ cups milk*

Combine soup and milk in a saucepan stirring until boiling. Combine with noodles and season with sea salt and pepper. Pour into a casserole dish and sprinkle with cheese. Bake in a 180C oven for 20 minutes.

# Chunky Dip Quiche

**Serves 6.  A tasty recipe from the lovely Clare Kill.**

- *1 sheet puff pastry*
- *5 eggs*
- *1 tub basil and cashew chunky dip*
- *1 cup grated tasty cheese*

Beat eggs well, add dip and ½ the cheese and stir.  Line a greased or paper lined quiche dish with pastry and add the filling, sprinkle with remaining cheese.  Bake in a preheated 180C oven for 30 minutes or until set.

*Optional:  Add chopped olives and sun-dried tomatoes if in your refrigerator.*

# Curry Noodle Bowl

**Serves 6**

- *3 x 85g instant noodles with vegetable flavouring*
- *4 cups liquid vegetable stock*
- *1 tbs. red curry paste*
- *500g pkt. mixed frozen stir fry veges,*
  *thawed (or you can also use mixed fresh veges)*

Break noodles in a bowl.  Combine seasoning packets, stock and curry paste in a large saucepan.  Add 2½ cups water and bring to boil, stirring regularly.  Add noodles and vegetables.  Cook for about 3 minutes, stirring occasionally until noodles are tender and vegetables are tender but crisp.

# Eggplant & Ricotta Pasta

**Serves 4**

- *120g jar char-grilled, marinated eggplant*
- *500g jar tomato and basil sugo (pasta sauce)*
- *375g penne pasta, cooked and drained*
- *200g fresh ricotta*

In a saucepan, add eggplant to sugo and simmer for 10 minutes until warm. Divide pasta between 4 bowls and top with sauce and ricotta.


# Field Mushroom and Garlic Pizza

**Makes 2. Recipe from Rodger Fishwick.**

- *2 pieces Turkish bread*
- *2 tsp. minced garlic*
- *1 cup field mushrooms, sliced*
- *½ cup mozzarella cheese*

Preheat oven to 180C. Place Turkish bread on a baking paper lined tray. Spread minced garlic over the bread and place the mushrooms on top. Sprinkle with mozzarella cheese and bake for 10 minutes.

# Frittata

**Serves 4.  A recipe by Katrina Price.**

- *6 eggs*
- *3 cups freshly chopped spinach*
- *1½ cups grated parmesan*
- *½ cup breadcrumbs*

Beat the eggs with a whisk until light and fluffy, add spinach, cheese and breadcrumbs, season to taste.  Line a baking tray with paper, pour in mixture and cook for 20 minutes at 150C.

*Optional:  Add cinnamon if desired.*


# Maltese Cheese Pie

**Serves 4-6.  A recipe from Ralph Buttigieg.**

- *2 sheets puff pastry*
- *500g ricotta cheese*
- *3 eggs*
- *¼ cup chopped parsley*

Combine the ricotta and parsley in a mixing bowl.  Beat the eggs and add to mixture, reserving a small amount to paint the top of the pie. Season with sea salt and pepper.  Line a greased, or paper lined pie dish, with one sheet of pastry.  Add the mixture and cover with remaining sheet, seal the edges with a fork and trim excess pastry.  Cut 2-3 air holes in the lid and baste with remaining egg. Bake in 180C oven for 30-35 minutes or until pastry golden on top.

# Polenta & Zucchini Lasagne

**Serves 6**

- *1 cup polenta*
- *2-3 zucchinis, grated*
- *575g jar of Creamy Tomato and Mozzarella pasta sauce*
- *2 cups grated mozzarella*

Add 1 cup of polenta to 4 cups of boiling water, stir frequently until thick. Remove and allow to cool for 5 minutes. Roughly, divide polenta into a quarter and use the first quarter to line the bottom of a rectangular baking dish. Cover the polenta with pasta sauce, zucchini and a third of the cheese, season. Continue for another 3 layers, ensuring last layer is mozzarella. Bake in a 180C oven for 30 minutes or until cheese is nice and brown on top. Enjoy with a yummy salad or roast veges!

*Optional: Substitute zucchini for whatever vegetable you like eg., mushrooms, sweet potato, baby spinach.*


# Potato Tortilla

**Serves 4**

- *¼ cup olive oil*
- *2 peeled and sliced potatoes*
- *8 eggs*

Heat olive oil in a fry pan over medium heat. Cook potatoes for 2-3 minutes. Whisk eggs together and season. Pour over potatoes and cook for a further 10 minutes. Place under a hot grill for 2 minutes or long enough to brown. Allow to cool before cutting into wedges to serve.

*Hint: To keep eggs fresh, store in fridge in their carton as soon as possible after purchase. This is because an egg will age more in a day at room temperature than it will in a week in the fridge.*

# Spinach & Ricotta Quiche

**Serves 4. A recipe by David Wilson.**

- *1 sheet puff pastry*
- *2 large eggs*
- *1½ cups ricotta cheese*
- *1½ cups shredded spinach*

Place pastry in a greased or paper lined quiche dish. Beat eggs, add ricotta and mix well. Add spinach and season with sea salt and pepper. Pour mixture into pastry and bake in 180C oven for 25 minutes or until set.


# Spinach Pie

**Serves 2. A recipe from Karyn Turnbull-Markus.**

- *2 cups shredded spinach*
- *250g cottage cheese*
- *2 eggs, whisked*
- *2 cloves garlic, crushed*

Boil spinach for 5 minutes, drain and then in a small oven proof dish, layer spinach, cottage cheese and garlic. After each layer, spoon over a little egg, continue until all ingredients are used, ensuring final layer is cottage cheese then season with cracked pepper. Bake in 180C oven for 20 minutes or until pie is slightly brown on top.

# Sweet Potato & Feta Frittata

**Serves 4.  A *fabulous* dinner for anyone.**

- *1 large orange sweet potato, peeled and cubed*
- *2 tbs. extra virgin olive oil*
- *200g feta, crumbled*
- *6 eggs*

Preheat oven to 200C.  Spread potato on a baking tray and sprinkle with half the oil.  Bake for 20 minutes or until tender.  Over medium heat, put remaining oil in a non-stick fry pan and add potato and feta.  Whisk eggs and season with sea salt and pepper then pour over potato and feta.  Reduce heat to low and cook for 5 minutes or until the base is set.  Place frittata under medium preheated grill (ensure a metal handle) for 7 minutes or until cooked through. Allow to cool slightly then cut into wedges.

*Optional:  This is delicious served with a fresh green salad.*


# Vege Stack

**Serves 2.  Recipe by beautiful Boofy.**

- *1 tortilla*
- *2 cups sweet potato (or pumpkin) cut into 1 cm strips*
- *2 cups grated cheese (or feta)*
- *2 large red capsicums cut into 4 cm strips*

Preheat oven to 180C.  Boil sweet potato for 10 minutes.  Sprinkle some water on capsicums and lay on a baking paper lined tray for 8 minutes or until capsicum is cooked.  Place tortilla in a round dish and layer with potato, capsicum and cheese alternatively.  Bake for about 35 minutes or until golden brown.

*Optional:  Serve with sweet chilli sauce or sour cream or you can also sprinkle some finely chopped garlic to the layers too.*

# Desserts

The best thing a Father can do for his children
is to love their Mother!

**Unknown**

---

## Apple Crumble

**Serves 6 ... Simply scrumptious!**

* *800g can sliced apples*
* *¼ cup sultanas*
* *220g pkt buttersnap biscuits, crushed*
* *½ cup butter, melted*

Preheat oven 180C.  Combine apple and sultanas, spoon into baking
dish.  Mix biscuits with butter and sprinkle over apple mixture.
Bake for 15 minutes or until golden and serve with cream or custard.

**Another delicious variation from Lorraine Leeson.**

* *800g tin pie apple*
* *½ cup melted butter (extra for greasing)*
* *½ cup brown sugar*
* *250g pkt scotch finger biscuits, crushed*

Lightly grease individual serving dishes.  Evenly layer apple into
each dish.  Cream butter and sugar until mixture is quite fluffy.  Mix
in biscuits then spread evenly over apple.  Bake for 30 minutes in a
180C oven until topping is golden.

*Optional:  Cinnamon may be added to biscuit mixture if desired.*

---

# Baked Apples with a Twist

**Makes 2.  A recipe by Rob Watson. "D.e.l.i.c.i.o.u.s!"**

- *2 granny smith apples*
- *1 Mars bar, frozen and cut in half*
- *2 tbs. Muscat wine/ liqueur*
- *1 tsp. brown sugar*

Core the apples so half the Mars bar fits into the middle, wrap in alfoil like a bomb, gently fill each with 1 tbs. muscat and sprinkle with sugar.  Bake in 180C oven (or on top of BBQ) for 20 minutes.  The muscat will poach the apple and the Mars bar *ooooozes* everywhere.

*Optional:  Serve with a scoop of ice-cream.*

# Baked Ricotta with Blueberry Sauce

**Serves 4.  Kim's favourite!  Dish this up to the *applause* of all!**

- *2 egg whites*
- *6 tbs. honey*
- *1 generous cup ricotta cheese*
- *2 cups frozen blueberries, thawed*

Preheat oven to 180C.  Beat egg whites until stiff peaks form.  Mix through 4 tbs. honey and ricotta cheese.  Once combined, pour into a small, baking paper lined, oven proof dish and bake for 40 minutes or until the pie rises and is golden.  Meanwhile, place the berries in a small frying pan and heat gently until softened.  Stir through 2 tbs. honey and allow to simmer for 20 minutes.  Serve blueberry sauce over ricotta pie wedges.

# Baked Rice Custard

**Serves 4 … This is really easy and really tasty!**

- *1/3 cup rice*
- *¾ cup condensed milk*
- *3 eggs, lightly beaten*
- *¼ cup sultanas*

Preheat oven 180C.  Cook rice in a large pan of boiling water for 10 minutes, drain.  Combine condensed milk, eggs, rice and sultanas with 1¾ cups water and mix thoroughly.  Pour into a shallow oven-proof dish.  Stand dish in baking pan with enough hot water to come halfway up sides of dish.  Bake for 40 minutes or until set.

*Optional:  Before baking sprinkle with nutmeg.*

# Bread & Butter Pudding

**Serves 4.  A yummy recipe from Ralth Buttigieg.**

- *2 tbs. butter*
- *4 slices cafe style raisin bread*
- *2½ cups milk*
- *2 tbs. Foster Clark's egg custard mix*

Butter the bread slices well and cut into fours.  Layer bread into a greased oven proof dish.  Mix the milk and custard powder until all the powder dissolves.  Pour over bread and allow at least ½ hour for the bread to soak up the liquid. Bake in a preheated 180C oven for 15-20 minutes or until the top is golden brown.  Allow to cool and enjoy!

*Optional:  Spread bread with your favourite jam as well.*

# Butterscoth Pumpkin Pie

**Serves 8 and is delightfully delicious!**

- *2 eggs*
- *375ml butterscotch ripple ice-cream, melted*
- *1¼ cups mashed pumpkin*
- *1 pie crust or bickie base*

Beat eggs until frothy. Add ice-cream and pumpkin. Stir until smooth. Pour filling into pie crust and bake in 180C oven for about 45 minutes or until the filling is set. Cool and enjoy!

*Optional: Can use English toffee ice-cream.*


# Caramel & Coconut Ice-cream

**Serves 8**

- *600ml cream*
- *380g can caramel top 'n' fill*
- *2 tbs. Bailey's liqueur*
- *¼ cup shredded coconut, toasted*

Combine cream, caramel and liqueur in large bowl and beat until thick and creamy with an electric mixer. Fold in coconut and pour into a paper lined baking tin, cover and freeze for at least 4-6 hours before serving.

# Caramel Pears

**Serves 4**

- *1 large tin pears*
- *2 tbs. butter*
- *¾ cup brown sugar*
- *1 tbs. lemon juice*

Put brown sugar, butter and lemon juice into large frying pan.
Stir over low heat until sugar dissolves, bring to boil, reduce heat,
simmer 2 minutes.  Add drained pears, cook for further 2 minutes.
Serve with ice-cream or cream.


# Caramel Walnut Tarts

**Makes 24.  Recipe from Marie McColl.**

- *1½  sheets shortcrust pastry, thawed*
- *380g tin caramel top 'n' fill*
- *½ cup smooth peanut butter*
- *1½  cups chopped walnuts*

Preheat oven 200C.  Cut full sheet into 16ths and half sheet into
8ths.  Press each square into non-stick mini-muffin trays.  Bake for
8-10 minutes or until just golden, allow to cool. Whisk caramel and
peanut butter until smooth, and add 1 cup walnuts and stir through.
Fill pastry cases with caramel mixture and sprinkle with remaining
walnuts.

# Choc-Caramel Ravioli

**Makes 16. Another from the talented Marie McColl.**

- *2 sheets puff pastry*
- *2 Snickers bars, cut 2cm thick*

Preheat oven 200C. Line a baking tray with baking paper.
Cut each sheet into 16 squares, place 2 slices of snickers on to
the first 16 squares. Top with remaining squares, seal all 4 edges
with a fork and trim excess pastry. Bake 10-12 minutes or until
puffed and golden.

*Optional: Delectable served with a creamy ice-cream.*


# Choc-Cherry Ice-cream Slice

**Makes 15. Recipe from the beautiful Rebecca Butler.**

- *2 x 200g pkt malt biscuits*
- *600ml thickened cream*
- *380g can condensed milk*
- *3 x 85g Cherry Ripe chocolate bars, roughly chopped*

Line a lamington tray (approx. 20cm x 30cm) with baking paper and
arrange a layer of bickies on its base. Beat cream with an electric
mixer just until soft peaks form, fold in condensed milk and Cherry
Ripes. Spread over bickies and top with another layer of bickies.
Cover with cling wrap and freeze overnight. Cut between bickies
to serve.

# Chocolate Mousse Patty Cakes

**Makes 6.  Recipe from Wendy King.**

- *250g milk chocolate*
- *3 eggs*
- *¼ cup flour*
- *1½ cups of whipped cream for serving*

Preheat oven to 180C.  Melt chocolate in a lightly heated saucepan stirring often to smooth.  Mix eggs and flour with whisk and stir into chocolate.  Place 6 patty cake papers into muffin tin and spoon in mixture.  Bake for 20 minutes or until sides are set but centre is still liquid. Cool 10 minutes. Carefully remove paper, centres will be a warm mousse consistency.  Top with a dollop of cream.

*Optional:  Sprinkle shaved chocolate on cream to make it look even MORE dazzling!  Also delicious served with the following ice-cream ...*


# Cookies & Cream Ice-cream

**A recipe from Jayne in WA ... In her words "YUM – This is my hubby's fave."**

- *380g tin condensed milk*
- *600 ml whipping cream*
- *200g high quality chocolate*
- *220g pkt plain chocolate bickies*

Melt chocolate in a microwave, stirring every 30 seconds.  Leave to stand and while cooling beat condensed milk and cream until thick, stir in melted chocolate and smashed bickies, pour into a paper lined tray, cover and freeze over night.

# Custard Tarts

**Makes 12**

- 2 sheets puff pastry, thawed
- 500g premium vanilla custard
- 3 tbs. brown sugar

Preheat oven to 200C. Cut 6 rounds from each sheet of pastry and line a non-stick muffin tray with them. Place a circle of baking paper with some uncooked rice on each and blind bake for 10-12 minutes. Remove paper and rice and allow to cool. Spoon an equal quantity of custard into each and sprinkle with brown sugar. Place tarts under a preheated grill allowing sugar to caramelise. Remove from heat and allow to cool slightly before serving.

*Optional: Another really lovely filling is caramel top 'n' fill. Blind bake as above and cool before scooping in well beaten caramel. Top with a dollop of freshly whipped cream and a fresh slice of strawberry or kiwi fruit.*


# Frozen Yoghurt Tarts

**Makes 16-20**

- 20 frozen mini tart shells, thawed
- 1 cup thick strawberry yoghurt
- ¾ of a 250g block cream cheese, softened
- ¾ cup strawberry jam

Place shells in 200C oven for 10 minutes or until golden brown and allow to cool. Beat remaining 3 ingredients until smooth. Spoon into tart shells and refrigerate for at least 2 hours.

*Optional: Instead of frozen mini tart shells, use a pkt of buttersnap bickies. Simply line a muffin tray with paper muffin shells and lay a buttersnap bickie flat side up and distribute evenly with mixture.*

# Little Lemon Cheesecakes

**Makes 8.  Kim's hubby Glen's new f.a.v.o.u.r.i.t.e!**

* *250g cream cheese, softened*
* *280g jar lemon butter*
* *8 butternut snap cookies*

Line 8 holes of a muffin tray with paper muffin shells and place a buttersnap bickie flat side up in each.  Using an electric mixer, beat cheese until creamy, then add all the lemon butter, mixing until nice and creamy.  Spoon mixture onto biscuits and freeze for 2-3 hours or until firm.  5 minutes before serving, remove paper and serve decorated with fresh seasonal fruit.

# Lime Sherbert

**Serves 6-8**

* *600ml cream*
* *380g tin of condensed milk*
* *1 lime*
* *3 egg whites*

Combine cream, condensed milk, 2 tsp. lime rind and ¼ cup lime juice in large bowl and beat until thick with an electric beater.  Beat egg whites until firm peaks form, fold into cream mixture.  Pour into a freezer pan, cover and freeze for at least 4-6 hours before serving.

*Optional:  If you don't have a freezer pan use a cake tin and line it with baking paper as it makes the ice-cream easier to remove and serve. Lime can be successfully substituted with lemon.*

# Lisa's Upside Down Pear Tart

**Serves 6.  A recipe from the gorgeous Lisa Darr.**

- *2 tbs. butter (a little extra for glazing)*
- *¼ cup real maple syrup*
- *2 firm pears, peeled*
- *2 sheets puff pastry*

In a frying pan, sauté butter and maple syrup until toffee like.  Place pears in toffee and coat well.  Cut a circle from puff pastry (enough to cover bottom of pan) and glaze both sides with a little melted butter, lay over pears.  Place frypan (ensure a metal handle) into a 180C oven and bake for 20 minutes or until pastry is crisp and golden.  Invert onto a serving plate and enjoy!

*Optional:  Serve with a dollop of cream or ice-cream.*


# Matchsticks

**Serves 4 … These are Kim's childhood favourites that continue to stand the test of time!**

- *2 sheets puff pastry, thawed*
- *1 cup cream, whipped*
- *4 tbs. strawberry jam*
- *2 tbs. icing sugar*

Roll out pastry, thinning it as much as possible.  Line two baking trays with baking paper and place a sheet of pastry on each.  Prick well and chill for 15 minutes in freezer.  Bake in 200C preheated oven for 8-10 minutes or until pale golden brown.  Using an egg flip, carefully turn pastry and bake for a further 6-8 minutes.  Remove from oven and allow to cool.  Cut both sheets into 4 lengthways (may get 5), spread the first sheet with jam and the second with cream and join together so that plain pastry faces up.  Top with a sprinkling of icing sugar … *Enjoy!*

# Peanut Butter Ice-cream Pie

**Serves 8-10 ... This IS  S.E.N.S.A.T.I.O.N.A.L!**

- *1 ltr. vanilla ice-cream, softened*
- *1¼ cups crunchy peanut butter*
- *1 pkt biscuit base mix*

Make the biscuit base mix as per instructions on packet and chill (generally it's as simple as adding melted butter).  Beat ice-cream and peanut butter in large bowl with an electric mixer until nice and smooth.   Pour into the biscuit base and place in freezer for at least 3 hours prior to serving.

*Optional:   Add 2 tbs. of cocoa or cinnamon to the biscuit base.  Serve drizzled with the Hot Fudge Sauce (see: Sauces)... Yummmmmmmmy!*


# Pineapple Flummery

**Serves 8 and is delicious!**

- *440g can crushed pineapple*
- *1 pkt lemon flavoured jelly crystals*
- *375ml can evaporated milk, chilled*

Drain juice from tin of pineapple.  Place juice and 1 tbs. cold water in a small saucepan over medium heat and bring to boil.  Place jelly crystals in a bowl and add boiling pineapple juice mixture.  Stir until jelly crystals dissolve.  Refrigerate for 20 minutes or until mixture is almost set.  With an electric mixer beat chilled milk for 4-5 minutes or until the consistency of whipped cream, wash beaters.
Beat jelly until frothy, then fold into thickened milk.  Pour into serving bowl, cover with cling wrap and refrigerate for an hour or until firm.

# Plum Pudding

**Serves 6.  A recipe from Daphne Beutel ... This is a XMAS KNOCKOUT!**

- *2 cups self raising flour*
- *1 cup sugar*
- *1 pkt fruit mix*
- *1 tbs. bicarbonate of soda*

Mix the first 3 ingredients together in a large bowl.  Mix 2 cups of hot water with bi-carb. of soda, add to the mixture and mix with a knife. Cover and leave overnight.  Mix well the next morning.  Place in a floured cloth and boil for 3 hours.

# Quick No-Fail Cheesecake

**A recipe by the very clever Michelle Steffensen!**

- *250g cream cheese, softened*
- *380g condensed milk*
- *Juice of 3 lemons*
- *A bought biscuit/tart base*

Bake base in 180C oven for 10 minutes or until golden brown.
Mix first 3 ingredients well and pour into the base.
Allow to set overnight.

*Optional:  Decorate with whipped cream, a passionfruit and the zest of a lemon!*

# Strawberry & Banana Skewers with Caramel Dip

**Makes 12 and is always *soooooooooooooooooo* popular!**

- *500g strawberries, washed and hulled*
- *2 bananas, peeled and sliced*
- *380ml tin top 'n' fill caramel*
- *1/3 cup cream*

Pour caramel and cream into a saucepan, bring to the boil and reduce heat simmering for 2 minutes. Pour mixture into jug, allow to cool. Thread strawberries and banana onto skewers and drizzle with caramel sauce when ready to serve.

*Hint: Always wash strawberries before you remove their stalks, otherwise water will get into the fruit and spoil their flavour.*


# Stuffed Apples

**Makes 4. *YUMMMMMMMMMMMMMMMY!!!***

- *4 large green apples*
- *1 cup leftover fruitcake or Christmas pudding*

Core apples and wrap in alfoil and bake in a 180C oven for 20 minutes. Remove alfoil and stuff with fruitcake, bake for a further 10 minutes. Serve warm with custard.

*Optional: Can sprinkle with cinnamon or substitute fruit cake for sultanas as Kim's Nana, Mary Moore, has been doing for decades!*

# Toblerone Mousse

**Serves 6.  Always a crowd pleaser!**

- 2 x 100g blocks dark Toblerone chocolate, broken
- 4 eggs, separated
- 300ml tub thickened cream
- 2 tbs. Tia Maria (optional)

Melt chocolate in microwave, stirring every 30 seconds.  Cool slightly.  Add in egg yolks.  Whip egg whites to a stiff peak.  Whip cream until stiff then fold into melted Toblerone.  Add egg whites and liqueur, fold until mixed.  Spoon mousse into serving dishes. Chill until set.

*Optional:  Serve with cream or ice-cream and fresh fruit.*


# Tropical Fruit Salad

**Serves 4.  *Divine!***

- 1 ripe mango, diced
- 8 lychees, peeled and quartered
- 1 banana, peeled and sliced
- 3 passionfruit

Combine all and mix.  Delicious served with ice-cream or as an accompaniment to a sweet.

# Yoghurt Ice-cream

**Serves 6-8.  A recipe from Joanne Mason.**

- *380g tin of condensed milk*
- *200ml tub banana yoghurt (or flavour of your choosing)*
- *300ml tub cream*

Mix well all ingredients in an empty ice-cream container and pop into the freezer overnight.  As an option, yoghurt can be replaced with banana, strawberries, mango or any fresh fruit you choose.


# Yummy Jaffa Parcels

**Makes 8**

- *2 sheets frozen puff pastry*
- *125g dark chocolate, broken*
- *1 orange*

Preheat oven to 200C.  Cut each pastry sheet into 4 quarters.  In a bowl,  combine chocolate, zest (from entire orange) and diced orange.  Place 2 tbs. of the mix in the centre of each sheet.  Lift each corner to cover the mixture forming an envelope, seal well.  Place on a paper lined baking tray and bake for 15 minutes or until golden.

*Optional:  Serve dusted with icing sugar and a dollop of ice-cream.*

# Drinks

The only man who never makes a mistake,
is the man who never does anything.

**Anonymous**

---

## Affogato

- *1 cup of your favourite hot, espresso coffee*
- *1 scoop of vanilla ice-cream*

This looks fabulous served in a glass.  Dollop ice-cream into coffee ... It may seem strange, but it's very yummy!

*Optional:  For an extra indulgence pour a little Baileys over the ice-cream.*

## Banana and Strawberry Smoothie

**Recipe by dynamic Nutritionist Cyndi O'Meara.**

- *1 cup milk (or natural yoghurt)*
- *1 banana*
- *6 strawberries*
- *1 tbs. honey*

Put all ingredients into a blender and mix until smooth.

# Berry Smoothie

- 1 cup frozen berries
- 2 cups chilled milk
- 4 scoops vanilla ice-cream

Blend until smooth.  Pour into tall glasses and serve.

# Blueberry Smoothie

- 1 cup frozen blueberries
- 2 cups chilled milk
- 4 scoops strawberry ice-cream

Blend until smooth.  Pour into tall glasses and serve.

# Green Fizz

- ¼ honeydew melon
- 1 kiwi fruit
- 2 cups lemon and lime mineral water

Blend melon and kiwi fruit.  Add mineral water and garnish with ice cubes and a slice of lime.

# Green Grape Smoothie

- *Slice of lime*
- *2 cups green seedless grapes*
- *1 cup diced pineapple*

Place ingredients in a blender with 1 cup cold water and 1 cup ice cubes, blend until smooth.  Pour into glasses and serve.


# Fruity Christmas Punch

**A recipe from Jennette McCosker served up to rave reviews each Xmas!**

- *2 punnets of strawberries, reserve a few*
- *1½ ltr. orange juice*
- *2 ltr. lemonade*


Puree strawberries and place in a bowl.  Stir in orange juice and with reserved strawberries, slice and add.  Mix in lemonade and serve over ice in tall glasses ... *Cheers Santa!!!*


# Lemonade

- *¾ cup lemon juice, freshly squeezed*
- *¼ cup sugar*
- *1¼ ltr. soda water*

Place juice and sugar in saucepan over low heat, stir until sugar has dissolved.  Simmer for 3 minutes to create syrup and cool in fridge.  Pour cold lemon syrup into a large jug over ice-cubes, top with soda water.  Stir before serving.

# Lychee Pineapple Cocktail

**A recipe from Julie Forato who says: "This recipe is a real winner – great for breakfast, brunch, lunch, or as a pre-dinner cocktail with a shot of vodka!"**

- *5 lychees with half a cup of syrup (from tin)*
- *15 mint leaves*
- *½ cup pineapple juice*
- *10 ice cubes*

Place all ingredients into a blender, and blend together until the ice is completely crushed. Serve in a glass garnished with mint leaves.


# Mango Smoothie

**Serves 2**

- *4 frozen mango cheeks*
- *2 cups cold milk*
- *1 tsp. ground cardamom*

Blend mango and milk until smooth. Pour into glasses, sprinkle with cardamom and serve.


# Marshmallow Hot Chocholate

**Makes 1**

- *1 tbs. drinking chocolate*
- *1 cup milk*
- *3 marshmallows*

For each serve blend drinking chocolate and milk in a saucepan. Add marshmallows and stir over heat until mixture almost boils. Pour into mug and enjoy!

# Mint Tea

**Makes 2**

- *8-10 fresh mint leaves*
- *2 slices lemon*
- *½ tsp. sugar*

Boil 2 cups of water and pour into a teapot. Add mint leaves and allow to infuse for 5 minutes. Serve with a slice of lemon and sugar to taste.

*Hint: A few finely chopped mint leaves will add a fresh flavour and fragrance to practically any cool soft drink.*

# Mud and Worms

**Serves 2. Recipe by Michelle Dodd who says "Try this on the kiddlies who don't drink milk ..."**

- *4 small scoops of chocolate ice-cream*
- *¼ cup milo*
- *1½ cups milk*
- *8 snakes*

Put 4 snakes into 2 tall, narrow glasses. Add 2 scoops of ice-cream and sprinkle with half the milo. Blend the remaining milo with the milk and pour over the ice-cream.

# Pineapple Banana Smoothie

**Serves 2**

- *1 cup orange juice*
- *1 cup pineapple juice*
- *2 frozen bananas*
- *2 dates, pitted*

Blend all ingredients until smooth and serve.

# Pineapple Tea Punch

**Makes 1½ litres**

- *1 ripe pineapple*
- *12 mint leaves*
- *2 cups cold black tea*
- *2 x 285ml of dry ginger ale*

Peel pineapple and remove core, chop roughly. Place half of the pineapple with half the black tea and mint leaves into a blender on high speed for 30 seconds. Add the remaining pineapple and black tea and blend for another 30 seconds. Refrigerate and just before serving add ginger ale.

# Sludgy Slime Shots

- 1 pkt of aeroplane jelly crystals
- 4 scoops of chocolate ice-cream
- 3 tbs. milk

Prepare jelly according to the packet instructions and leave to set for 30 minutes. Place the ice-cream and milk in a bowl and mash roughly with a fork until the ice-cream is soft. Layer small spoonfuls of ice-cream and jelly into 4 small glasses.

# Watermelon Refresher

- 1 kg seedless watermelon, coarsely chopped
- ¾ cup chilled orange juice, freshly squeezed
- 3 tbs. lime juice, freshly squeezed

Blend or juice. Garnish with lime slices.

*Optional: Grate in a tsp. of orange and lime zest.*

# If a Child Lives with Criticism

If children live with criticism, *they learn to condemn*
If children live with hostility, *they learn to fight*
If children live with fear, *they learn to be apprehensive*
If children live with pity, *they learn to feel sorry for themselves*
If children live with ridicule, *they learn to be shy*
If children live with jealousy, *they learn what envy is*
If children live with shame, *they learn to feel guilty*


If children live with tolerance, *they learn to be patient*
If children live with encouragement, *they learn to be confident*
If children live with praise, *they learn to appreciate*
If children live with approval, *they learn to like themselves*
If children live with acceptance,
 *they learn to find love in the world*
If children live with recognition, *they learn to have a goal*
If children live with sharing, *they learn to be generous*
If children live with honesty and fairness,
 *they learn what truth and justice are*
If children live with security,
 *they learn to have faith in themselves and in those around them*
If children live with friendliness,
 *they learn that the world is a nice place in which to live*
If children live with serenity,
 *they learn to have peace of mind.*

With what are your children living with?

**Dorothy L. Nolte**

# For The Children

Children will soon forget your presents,
they will always remember your presence.

**Dobson**

# Savoury

## Asparagus Rolls

**Makes 8**

- *8 slices wholemeal bread*
- *1 tbs. butter*
- *8 asparagus spears*

Remove crusts from bread and roll thin with a rolling pin. Lightly butter before placing an asparagus spear diagonally on each slice, roll tightly and cut in half.

## Basic Pizza Dough

- *1 sachet dried yeast*
- *½ tsp. salt*
- *2½ cups plain flour*
- *2 tbs. extra virgin olive oil*

Combine yeast and 1 cup warm water, cover and leave for 20 minutes. In a separate bowl, sift flour, add salt and make a well. Add the yeast mixture and oil. Mix with flat blade knife, using a cutting action, until a dough forms. Knead for 10 minutes or until smooth. Place in an oiled bowl, cover with cling wrap and leave for 45 minutes or until doubled in size.

# Chihuahuas

**Makes 6.  A favourite recipe by residents at Torbay Aged Care & Retirement Village Hervey Bay.**

- *6 (bake at home) mini bread rolls*
- *6 cheerios or chipolatas*
- *6 tsp. butter*
- *4 tsp. tomato sauce*

Immerse cheerios in boiling water until heated through (or if using chipolatas grill for about 10 minutes or until cooked).  Slice the rolls vertically and spread with some butter.  Insert sausage and drizzles with some tomato sauce and serve warm.


# Chicken Carnival Cones

**Makes 8.  A recipe by Isobele Whiting and enjoyed by *EVERYONE!***

- *8 flour tortillas*
- *2 cups leftover chicken meat, shredded*
- *ccup salsa*
- *1 cup grated cheese*

Fold tortilla in half (if small, fold only the bottom third up) and roll into a cone.  Fill bottom of cone with chicken, dollop 2 tsp. salsa before covering with a layer of cheese.  Place on a paper lined baking tray and repeat the process until all ingredients are used.  Bake in a 180C oven for 15 minutes.

# Chicken, Mango & Chickpea Burgers

**Makes 12**

- *400g chickpeas, drained*
- *500g lean chicken mince*
- *4-5 tbs. mango chutney*
- *2 shallots, finely chopped*

Process chickpeas, combine with remaining ingredients and season. Shape into patties and cook in a non-stick fry pan over a moderate heat for 3 minutes. Flip and cook for another 3 minutes or until cooked through. Serve on a fresh roll with a slice of tomato and lettuce.

# Chicken Nuggets

**Serves 2-4. They'll *loooove* them!**

- *2 chicken breasts, cut into nugget size pieces*
- *1 cup whole-egg mayonnaise*
- *1 cup seasoned stuffing mix*

Preheat oven to 180C. Coat chicken with mayonnaise and then roll in stuffing mix. Place on a paper lined baking tray and into the oven for 20 minutes.

# Easy Peasy Fish Cakes

**Makes 6.  A recipe from the lovely Robyn Mayeke.**

- *1 cup cooked, flaked fish*
- *1 cup mashed potato*
- *½ cup fresh or frozen peas*
- *1 egg*

Simply mix altogether, roll into balls and lightly pan fry.
Serve with salad.

# Easy Potato Bake

**Serves 2-4, depending on how hungry your children are!**

- *2 potatoes*
- *½ cup cream*
- *½ cup milk*
- *1 tbs. nutmeg*

Finely slice potatoes and layer in a greased pie dish.  Mix cream and milk together and pour over potatoes.  Sprinkle with nutmeg and bake in moderate oven for ½ hr or until golden brown.

# Frankfurt Pasta Bake

**Serves 4**

- *6 frankfurters, quartered*
- *2 cups cooked pasta spirals*
- *420g jar of pasta bake sauce*
- *1 cup grated cheese*

Preheat oven to 180C.  Mix frankfurters, pasta and sauce together, use only ¾ of the jar of sauce and add more if needed.  Spoon the mixture into a baking dish and sprinkle with cheese.
Bake for 20 minutes.

*Hint: Freeze remaining sauce for use at a later date.*


# Gourmet Sausages

**Serves 6.  A beauty from Marie McColl.**

- *6 of your favourite flavoured sausages*
- *2 sheets puff pastry, thawed*

Cut pastry into thirds, place a sausage at the edge of each and roll. Press the edge lightly with a fork to seal and cut excess pastry from lengths if necessary.  Bake in a 180C oven for 20-25 minutes or until pastry is nice and golden.  Slice into small bites and serve with favourite dipping sauce.

*Optional:  These are great served up as finger food at a BBQ as well!*

# Hummus Sausage

**Serves 2. Soooo quick and easy, recipe by the very suave Tony Van Dijk.**

- *4 herbed or Italian sausages*
- *4 tsp. hummus*
- *1 lemon, quartered*

Grill or sauté the sausage and serve with a dollop of hummus and a lemon wedge.


# Mini Cheese Quiches

**Serves 2. A recipe from the gorgeous Michelle Fredericks.**

- *6 slices of bread, crusts removed*
- *2 large eggs, lightly beaten*
- *½ cup grated cheddar cheese*
- *1 tbs. mixed herbs*

Press bread into non-stick muffin cups. Fill each cup with cheese and herbs and a sprinkle of pepper. Top each with egg mixture and bake in a 210C oven for 15 minutes or until set.


# Mouse Traps

**Serves 1. Recipe by Wendy King.**

- *2 slices day old bread*
- *1 slice shortcut bacon, cut in half*
- *2 slices tasty cheese*

Remove the sides off the bread. Lay a slice of cheese on each piece of bread and top with a slice of bacon on each. Place under grill and cook until bacon is crispy. Cut lengthways into 3 fingers and serve.

# Peanut Butter Toasties

**Serves 2**

- 2 slices wholemeal bread
- 2 tbs. peanut butter
- 2 tbs. sultanas
- ¼ cup grated cheese

Grill one side of the bread slices until golden. Turn and spread with peanut butter then sprinkle with sultanas and top with grated cheese. Grill until cheese is melted, cut in half to serve.

# Pine Tomato Chicken

**Serves 4**

- 8 chicken drumsticks, skinned
- 410g can of crushed or diced tomato
- 5 tbs. pineapple juice (use 90% plus juice)
- 3 tbs. of vinegar

Mix diced tomato, pineapple and vinegar together to make a marinade. Place chicken in a casserole dish and pour marinade over the top of each piece. Cover and refrigerate for 2 hours. Preheat oven to 220C, cover and cook chicken for around 40-50 minutes or until cooked throughout.
Serve with vegetables of choice.

# Savoury Fritters

**Makes 10**

- *1 pkt 2 minute chicken noodles*
- *4 eggs, lightly beaten*
- *2 shallots, finely chopped*
- *2 rashers bacon, chopped and lightly fried*

Cook noodles (without flavouring) then drain. Combine noodles with flavour sachet, eggs, shallots and bacon. Place egg rings in a non-stick fry pan and spoon enough mixture to fill the ring, cook on both sides until golden.

# Tacos

- *2 taco shells*
- *1 cup lean beef mince*
- *1/3 cup pasta sauce*
- *1 cup shredded lettuce*

Cook mince in a non-stick fry pan till pink has disappeared and add pasta sauce. Simmer on low heat for 5 minutes. Alternate a thin layer of mince with a thin layer of lettuce till each taco is full.

*Optional: You can also add sliced mushrooms, peas and shredded carrot to the mince meat mix too.*

# Tasty Fish

**Serves 5**

- *10 fish fingers*
- *320g can condensed tomato soup*

Preheat oven 180C.  Place fingers in a baking dish.
Cover with soup and bake for 45 minutes.
Serve with chips and veges.


# Yummy Bean Grill

**Makes 2**

- *130g can baked beans*
- *1-2 tbs. finely chopped parsley*
- *2 slices wholemeal bread, lightly toasted*
- *2 thin slices mozzarella cheese*

Combine beans and parsley and spread over toast.
Top with mozzarella and place under preheated grill
until cheese melts.

# Sweet

When buying chocolate, bear in mind that the higher the percentage of cocoa solids, the higher the quality of chocolate, and the less sugar it has.

**The best quality has 70% cocoa solids.**

## Basic Biscuits

**Makes about 72. "Very good value for money!"**

- *500g butter*
- *5 cups self raising flour*
- *1 cup sugar*
- *380g tin condensed milk*

Cream sugar and butter until white and fluffy. Sift in flour, and pour in condensed milk. Mix to combine. Roll into teaspoon size balls and place on paper lined baking tray. Flatten slightly with a fork. Bake in 180C oven for 10–12 minutes or until golden.

*Optional: Anything can be added to the basic mix to give variety, such as; smarties, cornflakes, sultanas, finely diced apple, cinnamon, choc chips etc. For a healthier version, use half wholemeal flour.*

*NB: Mixture will freeze. Roll into balls, and place in container layering with non-stick paper. Thaw slightly before cooking.*

# Bran Bars

- *6 cups Sultana Bran*
- *½ cup dried apricots, chopped*
- *¼ cup butter*
- *1 cup marshmallows*

Combine cereal and apricots in a bowl. Melt butter in a saucepan over medium heat. Add marshmallows, stirring until smooth. Pour over cereal and stir until coated. Press into a paper lined baking tin (approx 20 x 30 cm) and chill until firm. Slice ready for the lunchboxes.

*Optional: Any dried fruit can be used, is delicious with dried mango too! Alternatively they are nice set in patty papers.*


# Caramels

- *½ cup soft butter (plus a little extra for greasing)*
- *4 tbs. brown sugar*
- *2 tbs. golden syrup*
- *½ tin condensed milk*

Boil ingredients for 15 minutes, stirring frequently to prevent burning. Pour into a paper lined tin and when nearly set mark in squares. Cut when chilled.

# Caramel Biscuits

**Makes 20.  A recipe enjoyed by Riley Warrener and Liam Cooperthwaite.**

- *½ cup softened butter*
- *½ cup brown sugar*
- *2 tbs. golden syrup*
- *1 generous cup self raising flour*

Cream butter and sugar.  Add syrup and beat until fluffy.  Mix in flour until texture is such that you are able to roll into balls.  Place on a paper lined baking tray and allow for spreading, press each gently with a fork and bake in a 180C oven for 15 minutes.


# Caramel, Choc Truffles

**A recipe from Marie McColl ... They will be *devoured!***

- *380g can caramel top 'n' fill*
- *2 tbs. butter*
- *250g plain chocolate biscuits, crushed*
- *¾ cup desiccated coconut*

Combine caramel and butter in a pan, bring to boil stirring, remove from heat.  Add biscuit crumbs and mix well.  Refrigerate for 1 hour. Roll heaped teaspoons of mixture into balls, coat in coconut, chill until firm.

# Caramello Pears

**Makes 6.  Recipe by Kylie Burborough NZ ... Loved by 6 year olds *and* 60 year olds!**

- *3 ripe pears*
- *1 pkt caramel Rollos*

Preheat oven to 180C.  Cut the pears in half and core out seeds to make a shallow gully in the flesh.  Top with 2-3 caramel Rollos and bake until the chocolate has melted.

# Chocolate Scrunch

**Makes 18.  A recipe from Michelle Dodd.  Scrunch has a yummy crunchy texture and is super easy to make - kids love it and it goes well with coffee too!**

- *200g dark chocolate*
- *1 cup rice bubbles*
- *½ cup desiccated coconut*
- *¼ cup dried apricots, finely chopped, or other dried fruit*

Put the chocolate into a heatproof bowl, place over a pan of simmering water and stir frequently until the chocolate has melted. Fold in the rice bubbles, coconut and dried fruit and mix well.  Tip onto a paper lined baking tray and spread to a thin, even layer. Neaten edges then refrigerate till set. Cut into squares and enjoy!

# Date Slice

**A great sweet treat!**

- *1 cup chopped dates*
- *½ cup butter*
- *½ cup of caster sugar*
- *2 cups rice bubbles*

Bring 1½ cups of water to boil, add dates and boil for 5 minutes. Remove from heat and drain. Cream sugar and butter until smooth then add dates and rice bubbles. While warm press into a paper lined baking tin. Cut into squares and set in fridge.

# Fruit Dip

**Makes 1 cup**

- *1 cup natural Greek yoghurt*
- *½ tsp. ground cinnamon*
- *3 tbs. fruit jam*

Place all ingredients into a bowl and mix well. Chill for at least 2 hours prior to serving to allow flavours time to develop. Serve with a platter of fresh fruit for dipping.

# Fruit Medley

**Serves 8**

- *4 nectarines, chopped*
- *2 bananas, sliced*
- *1 cup blueberries*
- *1 tbs. orange juice*

Combine all ingredients in a bowl and gently toss.
Cool in fridge before serving.


# Hit The Road Bars

**Makes 12**

- *4 cups small rolled oats*
- *2 cups natural almonds, coarsely chopped*
- *320g condensed milk*
- *½ cup butter, melted*

Combine all ingredients in a large bowl and mix well.  Spread in a
well greased baking tin and bake in a 160C oven for 25 minutes or
until golden.  Allow to stand until slightly cooled then cut while still
warm.

# Jaxson's Double Choc Strawberries

**Makes 12.  This is fantastic for little kids and big kids!!!**

- *A big punnet of strawberries, washed*
- *½ cup dark chocolate*
- *¼ cup white chocolate*

Place strawberries in the fridge to chill.  Melt dark and white chocolate separately.  Dip strawberries in the dark chocolate ¾ the way up to the top of the chocolate – put back in fridge to solidify the chocolate.  Dip the chilled choc dipped strawberries into the white chocolate about 1 cm up so it's just covering the strawberry tips. Serve chilled.


# Jam Drops

**Makes 60.  Recipe by Joy Duke.**

- *1 cup butter, softened*
- *½ cup caster sugar*
- *2 cups plain flour*
- *Jam of choice*

Cream butter and sugar until light and fluffy.  Fold in flour and spoon into heaped dollops onto a paper lined baking tray.  Use the end of a wooden spoon to push a hole nearly to the base of the biscuit dough.  Fill hole with jam of choice and bake for 15 minutes or until slightly golden.  Remove from oven and allow to cool before serving.

*Optional:  Dust with icing sugar to jazz them up a bit for adult afternoon teas.*

# Jelly in Oranges

**Makes 6 and is a sparkling dessert at children's parties!**

- *3 ripe oranges*
- *1 pkt red jelly, set*

Cut oranges in half, remove flesh and fill with jelly.

*Optional: Top with a little ice-cream and sprinkle with 100's and 1,000's.*


# Mallow Pears

**Makes 4. A recipe by our lovely Aunty Nikki Ogawa.**

- *2 pears, halved and deseeded*
- *8 marshmallows*
- *¼ tsp. nutmeg*

Place pear halves on a microwave safe dish and cover with glad wrap. Microwave for 1 minute. Remove and top each pear with 2 marshmallows and a sprinkle of nutmeg. Grill under moderate heat until marshmallows are golden brown. Serve warm.

# Melon Ice Blocks

**Makes 5 cups**

- *4 cups chopped, seedless watermelon*
- *2 cups chopped fresh pineapple*

Combine all ingredients and blend, in batches, until smooth. Pour into iceblock moulds and freeze.

*Optional: Watermelon can be substituted with 2 cups of honeydew melon.*

# Peppermint Chocolate Slice

**Makes around 21 pieces. This is BRILLIANT and so very easy the kids can do it!**

- *1 pkt dark chocolate melts*
- *3 drops peppermint essence*
- *½ pkt white chocolate melts*
- *4 drops green food colouring*

Line 20cm square cake tin with baking paper or alfoil. Melt dark chocolate melts in a lightly heated saucepan, stirring throughout melting process. Add peppermint essence and stir. Spread half the mixture evenly over bottom of tin. Set in fridge for 5 minutes. Melt white chocolate melts the same way then stir in green food colouring. Spread this over layer of dark chocolate and then refrigerate until set. Spread remaining dark chocolate over white/ green chocolate and set in fridge. Cut into pieces and store in fridge.

*Hint: To make fun ice cubes for a party, add a drop or two of food colouring to the ice cube tray, you can make different colours for a pretty rainbow effect.*

# Raisin Dainties

**Makes 12**

- *2 cups cornflakes, crushed*
- *½ cup coconut*
- *1 cup raisins*
- *380g tin condensed milk*

Mix all ingredients well. Line a patty tin with patty papers and evenly distribute mixture. Bake in a 160C oven for 15 minutes or until nicely browned.

# Trail Mix

**Recipe from Lea Van Dijk.**

- *4 cups mixed nuts*
- *1 cup raisins or sultanas*
- *1 cup of dried apricots, chopped*
- *250g dark chocolate, chopped into various sized pieces*

Mix all together and store in cool area. Can also place into zip lock bags ready to grab and go.

# Vanilla Choc Dip

**Makes 1½ cups**

- *2 tubs vanilla fruche*
- *1 flake*

Crumble flake into vanilla fruche and serve with a fruit platter for dipping.

# Vanilla Ice-cream

**A terrific little recipe by the gorgeous Carly Nelson.**

- *4 cups cream*
- *4 cups full cream milk*
- *2 tbs. vanilla*
- *1½ cups of raw sugar*

Mix all ingredients together until thoroughly combined. Place in freezer for at least 4 hours prior to serving. Easy *and* cheap!

*Optional: Mix in some flaked chocolate or fresh fruit for variety – everyone will love it!*


# Yogo Tropo

**Serves 1. Recipe by the beautiful Maddie Willson created for a school assignment.**

- *1 Kiwi fruit, peeled and diced*
- *6 strawberries, washed, hulled and halved*
- *½ a banana, sliced*
- *200g tub vanilla yoghurt*

Into a glass place a layer of strawberries, top with a dollop of yoghurt, then a layer of kiwi fruit, a dollop of yoghurt, a layer of banana, strawberries and kiwi fruit and a final dollop of yoghurt. Decorate with leftover fruit and serve.

*Optional: Maddie says "To make it look jazzy serve with an open Hawaiian umbrella."*

# Think Inside The Box

An investment in knowledge always pays the best interest.

**Benjamin Franklin**

---

We all know it is imperative children get the right nutrients during the day to help sustain high levels of concentration and energy ... Yet often we struggle to make lunch boxes fun, healthy and eaten!

Given that lunch provides around one quarter of a child's daily nutritional requirements, it's in their best interests to fuel their bodies with great growing food and in our best interests to know they actually eat what is given to them.

Remember, where possible try to balance meals and lunch boxes so that children have something from each food group.

The food groups are:

1. **Bread, cereals, rice, pasta, noodles**
2. **Vegetables and legumes**
3. **Fruit**
4. **Milk, yoghurt, cheese and fish**
5. **Meat, poultry, eggs, nuts and legumes**

*For example;* a wholemeal sandwich with chicken, cucumber and cheese, a quartered orange, carrot sticks and yoghurt covers all the bases.

To keep children interested, change what you place in their lunchboxes each day. As well as providing carbohydrate, protein and healthy fat, this will ensure a diverse range of nutrients to keep those beautiful little bodies in peak condition inside and out.

# Sensible Lunchbox Tips

Here are some tips gathered from many a wise Mum at our children's schools and kindergartens that may just help.

- Buy a lunchbox that is airtight so you don't have to wrap food in plastics and foils.

- Such lunchboxes also allow you to make sandwiches the night before and store in the fridge. They will stay as fresh as if they were in wrapping.

- If your school or kindy doesn't have a fridge, place lunchboxes and drink bottles into an insulated lunch bag to keep cool.

- Alternatively use a frozen brick.

- Try to chill cooked foods such as egg, bolognaise etc. before packing (the zone for bugs to start is 50C - 60C so ensure all food is kept well below this temperature range).

- Encourage children to swish their water around their mouths after eating to briefly wash their teeth.

- Add a piece of sliced cheese to lunches, especially when you have included something a little naughty. Cheese will help to protect teeth from decay.

- Don't give your child nuts or foods that need supervision if you are unsure whether they are being watched over while they eat.

- Peel a pear or apple and soak in water that has the juice of ½ a lemon for a few minutes, it won't turn brown.

# Lunchbox Sushi

**Serves 2.  Presents beautifully and are very popular in our households!!!**

- *4 slices soy and linseed bread*
- *1 tbs. whole egg mayonnaise*
- *½ avocado, mashed*
- *½ cucumber*

Remove crusts and, with a rolling pin, gently roll bread to flatten slightly.  Along the middle of each slice spread a little mayonnaise and avocado.  Place long, thin strips of cucumber on top and roll tightly.  Cut in thirds, turn up and place into lunchbox for later.

*Optional:  Use a variety of breads.*

Other yummy fillings:
- Cream cheese, salmon and thin slices of cucumber
- Vegemite and thin slices of cheese
- Ham, cheese and finely shredded lettuce
- Cottage cheese, thinly sliced carrot and sultanas
- Peanut butter and thinly sliced carrot
- Egg and lettuce
- Grated apple, sultanas and cream cheese
- Tuna, mayonnaise and finely shredded lettuce
- Curried egg
- Avocado, shredded chicken and cheese

For a sweeter variety do the same as above but use fruit or raisin loaf slices and fill with the following;
- Strawberry jam and cream cheese
- Peanut butter and honey
- Mashed banana
- Peanut butter and mashed banana
- Nutella and grated apple
- Pineapple
- Peanut butter and strawberry jam
- Cottage cheese, jam and sultanas

# Skyscraper Sandwiches

**Serves 2.  Morgan McCosker looooves these in his lunchbox!**

- *6 slices bread*
- *2 slices cheese*
- *2 slices ham*
- *½ cup shredded lettuce*

Remove crusts and on two pieces of bread place a slice of cheese and ham.  Cover with another piece of bread, add lettuce and top with final slice of bread. Cut each in half and stack one on top of another to form two skyscraper sandwiches!

*Optional:  Vary the fillings to whatever your children will eat.*

# For The Baby

Wherever possible – breastfeeding is the best source of nutrition for your child, so it's best to feed for as long as you can. When your child is ready to transfer to solids, introduce lumpy foods after three to five weeks of pureed food. Gradually make it lumpier because this will help baby learn to chew even if he has no teeth. Add finger foods thereafter. By the time baby reaches his first birthday he should be eating regular family food with some modifications.

## Avocado Dip with Goats Cheese

**Recipe by our very clever chiropractor Dr Sarah Farrant.**

* ½ avocado
* 1 tbs. goats cheese
* 1 tbs. tomato sauce
* A squeeze of lemon juice

Blend all ingredients until thin in consistency. Serve to baby on a teaspoon.

## Avocado Yoghurt

* ¼ avocado, mashed well
* 1 tbs. yoghurt

Mix both well and serve immediately.

*Optional: Replace yoghurt with orange juice and add 1 tsp. rice cereal mix well and serve immediately.*

# Baby Meatballs

**Recipe by Janelle McCosker.**

- *250g lean mince*
- *½ cup mashed potatoes*

Preheat oven to 180C. Combine ingredients and mix well. Roll into little balls and place on baking tray and cook for around 20 minutes. Drain of excess liquid then cool and serve.

*Optional: Grate in some zucchini or a little cheese.*


# Banavo

**Recipe by Kim Morrison … They are sure to *looooove* this one!**

- *¼ avocado*
- *¼ banana*
- *½ tsp. manuka honey*

Mash well together and serve.


# Fruit Gel

- *1 sachet gelatine*
- *½ cup fruit juice*

Dissolve gelatine in ½ cup boiling water, add fruit juice and mix well. Pour mixture into a bowl and cover, cool and store in refrigerator to set.

# Fruity Teething Treat

**Rachael made these throughout the time Jaxson teethed and it was heaven on a stick for him!**

- *1 punnet strawberries, hulled*
- *2 cups diced watermelon*
- *2 apples, cored and sliced*
- *½ mango*

Blend all ingredients well and freeze into ice cube trays with paddle pop sticks inserted into each when half frozen. The children can hold onto them and suck away on the frozen fruit, it's nutritious and soothing all at the same time!

# Orange Delight

**Makes 2. Recipe by Cyndi O'Meara – perfect for an after school summer snack!**

- *2 oranges*

Insert a paddle pop stick into a peeled orange and freeze for an hour or 2.

# Prune Juice

- *12 prunes*

Soak prunes in water for 2 hours. Strain liquid into a saucepan. Bring to boil and add prunes. Reduce heat and simmer for 10 minutes or until tender. Strain juice and store in a sealed container in the fridge.

# Pumpkin Soup

**Pumpkin - a yummy baby food.  Loaded with Vitamin A and other nutrients.**

- *250g pumpkin, peeled and chopped*
- *¼ tsp. nutmeg*
- *½ cup cooked rice*

Place all ingredients in a saucepan with 2 cups of water, cover and bring to boil.  Reduce heat and simmer for 15 minutes or until tender.  Blend until smooth.

*Optional:  Use 2 cups of homemade stock if desired and substitute pumpkin for any vegetable.*

# Quick & Easy Cheese Sauce

**Makes 1 cup**

- *8 tbs. cream cheese, softened*
- *4 tbs. grated parmesan cheese*
- *1/3 cup milk*
- *Pinch nutmeg*

Place the cream cheese, parmesan and milk in a suitable dish and microwave on medium for 6-8 minutes, stirring every 2.  When the sauce is smooth, stir in the nutmeg.  Toss the sauce with hot, cooked pasta.

# Savoury Vegetables

**A recipe from Lisa Darr.**

- *1 cup mashed potato and pumpkin*
- *¼ tsp. vegemite*
- *2 tbs. grated cheese*

Mix all together whilst potato and pumpkin are warm and serve.


# Sweet Pear Puree

**A recipe from Wendy Beattie who said "Pears are often referred to as a hypoallergenic fruit and are recommended as a safe way to start feeding your baby solids."**

- *1 pear*
- *1 tsp. brown sugar*

Peel pear and remove top. Sprinkle with brown sugar and bake for 3 minutes. Mash, cool and serve.


# Sweet Potato & Fruit Mash

**A favourite in Kim's household.**

- *1 green apple, peeled and chopped*
- *200g sweet potato, peeled and chopped*
- *6 plump blueberries*

Place apple and sweet potato in a saucepan with 1½ cups water and boil until tender. Add blueberries and puree, serve warm.

*Optional: Add corn from a corn on the cob, that has also been boiled, to the mix before pureeing.*

# Vegeblend

- *1 cup pumpkin (or sweet potato)*
- *1 cup carrot*
- *1 cup broccoli*

Steam all vegetables then either mash or blend well with ¼ cup of breast milk or pasteurized only milk.

## And LOTS and LOTS of fresh fruit and raw vege sticks – start them early on the good stuff!

# For The Pet

"We can judge the heart of a man
by his treatment of animals."

**Immanual Kant**

---

## Birdie Breakfast Cereal

- ¼ cup instant oatmeal
- 1 tsp. peanut butter
- ¼ cup chopped apples or oranges

Place oatmeal in a microwave safe dish, cover with water and microwave on high for 1 minute. Remove the bowl, stir until the water is absorbed and the oatmeal is soft and cooked through. Add peanut butter and stir until dissolved. Stir in the fruit, allow to cool, stir and serve.

## Bird Sandwich

- 1 slice wholegrain bread
- 1 jar fruit baby food
- ½ cup chopped fruit or nuts

Spread baby food on wholemeal bread and add chopped fruit, vegetables or nuts.

*Optional: Substitute fruit for jar of vegetable baby food and ½ cup chopped veges for fruit.*

# Kitty Delight

- *1 can tuna*
- *½ cup milk*
- *1 can wet cat food*
- *1 cup white rice*

Cook the white rice until soft, add all other ingredients and stir until well blended.

# Mini Morsels for Mature Cats

- *1 can sardines, packed in olive oil*
- *1 cup wholegrain bread crumbs*
- *1 egg, beaten*

Pour contents of sardines in a medium bowl. Using a fork, mash into tiny pieces. Add remaining ingredients and mix well. Drop ¼ tsp. of mixture onto a paper lined baking tray and bake in a 150C oven for 7 minutes. Store in airtight container.

# Dog Biscuits

- *250g liver*
- *2½ cups plain flour*
- *2½ cups wheat meal*
- *1 cup bran*

Preheat oven to 200C. Place liver in a saucepan and cover with water, bring to the boil. Mince it and add remaining ingredients, mix well. Roll out and cut into thick slices. Bake for 10 minutes.

# Mint Rice Hamburgers

- 5 cups uncooked rice
- 10 cups water
- 1kg low fat hamburger mince
- 5 tbs. dried mint

Place rice and water in a large saucepan, bring to the boil. Add hamburger mince and mint and bring back to boil. Mix well. Reduce heat to low and simmer until all the water is absorbed. This is a great dinner for doggy halitosis!

# Fish Food

- 1, 3cm x 3cm piece of pumpkin

A small seeded, peeled piece of pumpkin dropped into a fish tank will delight fish. It floats and takes about three days to eat.

# Fish Cheerios

- 1 cheerio, finely chopped

Ensure very small pieces so as to avoid your fish choking. Place small amount in fish tank and freeze the remaining.

# Leftover Ideas

These are all fabulous ideas!   But you should be aware that it takes energy to run large fridges and freezers so the first solution to utilise leftovers and minimise waste, should always be to shop to a menu and only buy what you are going to use!

**Many Thanks to Carolyn Markham
of Bondi, NSW who inspired this section.**

## Leftover Chicken Ideas

**Chicken & broccoli casserole for one**: ½ kg fresh or frozen broccoli, 1cup shredded leftover chicken, ½ cup cream of chicken soup, ¼ cup parmesan cheese.  Preheat oven to 180C. Cook broccoli in boiling salted water.  Drain.  Grease a small casserole dish, place broccoli over bottom, top with chicken, pour over soup and sprinkle with parmesan.  Bake for 10-15 minutes or until lightly browned and bubbling.

*Optional:   Add ¼ tsp. cayenne pepper to soup.*

**Chicken & egg drop soup:**  Heat one cup of water to boiling on the stove, add 1 chicken stock cube, stir to dissolve.  Take 1 egg and whisk it in a separate bowl. Using the whisk again, gently stream the egg into the boiling broth, reduce heat and gently stir.   Add leftover shredded chicken and a vege or two, simmer until ready.

**Chicken stir fry:**  1 cup shredded leftover chicken, 1 tbs. sesame oil, 3 tbs. your favourite BBQ sauce.  Heat oil in wok until hot, add BBQ sauce and mix until combined.  Add chicken.  Lower heat and cook until almost done (add more sauce if you like).  Add vegetables and stir to cook for 3 minutes or to desired tenderness.

*Optional: You can make this vegetarian by omitting the chicken and adding tofu, nuts or even more veges.*

**Chicken tacos or burritos:** Shred leftover chicken and 1-2 tsp. of your favourite BBQ sauce, chill until sauce is completely absorbed in the chicken. Then make your own tacos or burritos with whatever salad your children will eat!

*Optional: Works just as nicely with left over mince.*

**Shred leftover chicken:** And mix with mayo, chopped tomato and fresh basil for a great sandwich filling.

# Leftover Fish Ideas

**Chop leftover tuna/fish patties:** And mix with a dollop of mayonnaise. Place in a wrap for lunch and top with freshly shredded lettuce leaves.

**Cook salmon or prawns:** Can easily be turned into fishcakes by mixing with mashed potato, mayo and fresh herbs. Pan fry until crisp and serve with a dollop of aioli.

**Fish:** Make a seafood sauce to have with pasta or rice.

**Fish toasties:** Flake leftover fish on top of toast. Top with cheese and grill. Cut into fingers and serve warm ... Great for the kids!!

**Fish cakes:** To leftover fish simply add mashed potato and an egg and mix well. Flavour with your choice of fresh herbs and spices, roll in breadcrumbs and bake or fry.

*Optional: Serve with an easy dipping sauce made by combining equal parts of sweet chilli sauce and honey (add coriander if avaliable).*

# Leftover Meat Ideas

**Dice the ham:** Add cold cooked green peas, cubed cheddar cheese and season with sea salt and pepper. Mix together with a bit of mayo.

*Optional: Add a little diced onion.*

**Ham bone:** Is very useful in adding flavour and thickening a pot of ham and pea or ham and bean soup.

**Leftover curries, sauces, soups:** Can be frozen - even if it's only enough for one portion, it's a solution for nights when you're home alone (and cheaper than takeaway!)

**Leftover roast pork:** Finely slice and stir fry pork with garlic, ginger, snow peas, roasted peanuts and soy sauce.

**Lunch:** Have a slice of ham on crunchy bread with Swiss cheese and grainy mustard.

**Meatloaf:** Spread fruit chutney and grated cheese over leftover meatloaf, then wrap in a sheet of puff pastry before baking in the oven ... *Scrummy!*

**Ham mix:** Chopped green capsicum and onions with cheese for a nice omelette.

**Stir fry beef mince:** With paprika, then add a can of tomatoes and kidney beans for a Mexican tortilla or nachos topping.

**Mince:** To half a kilo of mince add 1 packet of taco seasoning and shape into meatballs. Pour 2 tbs. olive oil into a frying pan and heat, brown meatballs, drain and serve in pita bread or burrito with salad and salsa.

# Leftover Rice Ideas

**Rice cakes:** Add 1 egg and ½ cup fresh breadcrumbs to leftover rice. Form into patties and fry in extra virgin olive oil until nice and golden.

**Risotto balls:** Roll tbs. of leftover rice or risotto into balls. Push a small cube of mozzarella into the centre and roll in breadcrumbs. Bake in a moderate oven for 10-15 mins. Balls can be shallow fried if you are in a hurry.

*Hint: In all the rice recipes, use moistened hands so that the rice doesn't stick.*

**Surplus cooked rice:** Cook with chopped vegetables, cashews, eggs or diced bacon. Add some soya sauce and you have a yummy fried rice.

*Optional: Also nice with a squirt of sweet chilli sauce.*

**Stuffed capsicums:** Leftover risotto, or other grain-based dishes like couscous can become a base for stuffed capsicums. Just add your favourite freshly chopped herb to it prior to baking.

**To cold rice add:** Grated lemon and parsley, parmesan and nutmeg or chopped olives and lemon rind. Roll into little balls, dip in seasoned flour and beaten egg and roll in fresh breadcrumbs. Gently fry in oil until crisp and golden. Drain.

# Leftover Vegetable Ideas

**Add leftover veges:** To risotto, chop roughly and stir through at the end of cooking with grated cheese.

**Baked potato toppings:** Chop leftovers finely, add them to baked potato and top with sour cream and cheese.

**Beetroot:** Place contents of opened canned beetroot in an airtight container and fill with a mixture of water and white vinegar. Refrigerate until needed, this helps keep beetroot fresh.

**Bubble and squeak:** Mash leftover veges, mix with a dollop of leftover gravy or tomato sauce and fry in lots of hot oil.

**Capsicums:** That are showing their age are shoved whole into the oven to roast, they are delicious in dips (see Red Yoghurt Dip) and soups (see Capsicum and Chorizo Soup) … yummo!!

**Fresh herbs:** Can be frozen if not used in time - defrosted, they're still OK in cooked dishes.

**Fritters:** Kim and Rachael's Mums have been making these for years! Perfect your classic fritter batter; 1¾ cups self raising flour, ½ cup milk, 1 egg, salt 'n' pepper … mix to quite a stiff batter and add to it whatever you want. Fry in lots of hot oil when ready.

*Optional: For a variation, and if in your cupboard, season with a pinch of curry powder or Tabasco sauce etc.*

**Grilled leftover veges:** Arrange leftover vegetables in one layer in an ovenproof dish. Cover with 3-4 slices of Gruyere cheese and grill until cheese has melted and veges are warm.

---

**Mashed for baby:**  Mashing leftover veges makes an ideal dish for baby's dinner.

**Potato chips:**  To crisp up leftover potato chips, wrap them in a single layer of kitchen paper towel and microwave on high for 30 seconds.

**Tasty mashed potatoes:**  Spoon leftovers into a dish, top with cheese, chopped bacon and paprika.  Bake at 210C for 10-12 minutes.

**Vegetable based dips:**  eg., hummus can be divided into portions so half can be frozen if they won't be consumed quickly.

**Wilted vegetables:**  Inevitably gather on the bottom of the fridge but can make a great soup with some leftover pasta and stock thrown in!

# Other Leftover Ideas

**Bread crusts:** Use leftover crusts by dipping them in melted butter, coating with finely grated cheese, then lightly sprinkling with curry powder. Cook in 200C oven, until crisp and browned. Great served with dips.

**Fruitcake:** Use leftover fruitcake in rum balls (4 ingredients) and stuffed, baked apples (4 Ingredients 2.)

**Leftover fruit:** Anything wrinkling or over ripe becomes stewed fruit to eat with yoghurt, muesli or stirred into porridge - except for bananas, mangoes or strawberries which are frozen for later use in baking.

**Plum pudding:** Fry slices of plum pudding in a little unsalted butter for 2 minutes on each side. Serve warm with custard or ice-cream.

**Stale cereals and nuts:** Pop them on a plate and microwave on high for 40 seconds. Then set aside to cool and crisp up.

**Leftover liquid from canned fruit:** Boil it until it's reduced by half. Add seasoning and use it to baste chicken. It tastes delicious and will keep the chicken moist.

**Left over wine:** Freeze wine into ice cube trays and use in cooking.

**Spaghetti Bolognaise:** On a sheet of puff pastry, spread bolognaise leaving a 2cm border. Top with baby spinach and grated parmesan cheese. Roll up the sheet and glaze with a beaten egg. Place on a paper lined baking tray and bake in at 200C oven for 20 minutes or until golden.

# Making More Time For You!

## By Rachael Bermingham

If there's one thing I know something about it's about how to fit in all the things I want to do into a single day. It hasn't always been the case though, and I must say, it never came naturally: In fact many years ago I had to learn it and let me tell you it was quite easily one of the most challenging things I ever did - but also one of the most beneficial too!

Fortunately I persisted, as it's been invaluable in enabling me to do everything I've wanted to do. In the past 3 years I've managed to run 2 businesses solo and co run 2 others from my home office during my gorgeous little boy Jaxson's sleep time. For 1½ years of that time (while I co wrote 2 books) my husband worked away on shifts ranging from 5 days on 4 off, to 11 days on 3 off. As a result whenever I am speaking at a seminar, people always ask 'How do you fit it all in?' After all it doesn't matter who you are, what your family circumstances are, we are ALL busy. It's just working out how to maximise that 24 hour period so it works for you rather than against you. So I thought I'd share some of my tips, from one busy person to another. I hope they are as helpful to you as they have been to me so you can spend more time for YOU!!

**1. GET A DIARY OR SCHEDULE.** This is not only a FANTASTIC resource for managing your time, but it also helps you to remember everything important  and allows you to see what you have in your day already so you don't over commit.

**2. PLAN.** I believe this is the single most important part in achieving anything and for clawing back some much needed YOU time. Spend some time planning what you want to do so you know what steps you need to take and when. This assists you in making relevant choices that move you closer to your goals.

**3. PRIORITISE.** Work out what is important to you and ensure you allocate plenty of time for those things first. For example my husband and son are my very first priority. So everything to do with them I schedule in first, friends come a very close second followed by business, then me and then the household. This may be different for you so you simply need to schedule according to what you see as important in your life.

**4. BE RUTHLESS.** I was always what I call a YES person. Whenever someone asked me to do something I'd say 'YES!' Howeeevvveerrrrr this always left me highly over committed and usually stressed! My diary is a great tool for helping me to be ruthless with my time. When someone asks if I can do something I say 'sure, let me check my schedule' and I'll see where I can slot the activity in. If it's next week or in 5 months time I am comfortable about responding and KNOW that if my 24 hours is booked up then it's booked up – if you work with it, it makes life a whole lot easier.

**5. OUTSOURCING WHAT YOU PROCRASTINATE ON.** We've all got our strengths (and just quietly, our weaknesses too). My weakness is in MYOB data entry. I know it rings some people's bells, but not mine. I wasn't blessed with administrative talent for it. It's not that I can't do it – I simply don't enjoy doing it. I know, without a shadow of doubt, that if left up to me, everything would wait until the last possible date when I would then find myself working like a mad woman to get it all updated in time. So to alleviate any stress or costly mistakes, I have a bookkeeper who is simply sensational and LOVES, LOVES, LOVES doing it and does it incredibly well. I'm happy, she's happy and the tax man is happy so everyone wins and we're all doing the things we love rather than stressing over what we don't.

**6. MINIMISE UNECESSARY TASKS.** Before I did get organised, one thing you would find me doing CONSTANTLY was going to the supermarket every other day to get ingredients for dinner. Often it would be a costly trip. 1/ because I'd go in without really thinking what we were having for dinner so would end up with a variety of ingredients I didn't even get to use, and 2/ because I was wasting time and fuel in doing it!  So if you can plan your weekly shopping menu and add all the required ingredients to your list then you won't have to visit the supermarket more than once a week, you save time travelling back and forth AND you save money too! *Happy Days!!!*

**7. USE COMPUTER TIME EFFECTIVELY.** We've probably all been guilty of a little out of school internet surfing right?  But it's one of THE biggest time zappers around.  One site leads into another and another etc, before you know it 2 hours has slipped away from you. The other time zapper is emails.  If you find yourself checking emails every 10 minutes or whiling away the hours in cyberspace, then a great tip I utilise is to allocate time for computer research and also emails. I book a block of time for research and also check emails 3 times throughout the day;  first thing in the morning, after lunch when Jaxson is sleeping and again when he goes to sleep at night and only on my work days, never on my days off.  This was really challenging to get used to, but it's sensational when you get the hang of it.  You can fit in far more to your day.

**8. ALLOCATE A BUFFER ZONE.**  We all have unexpected things that come up. Friends pop in, someone needs you to help them urgently, a job takes a little longer, transport is delayed, you slept in, or sometimes you just didn't feel like doing something that you had to do (which often masquerades the fact that you need to take a little time out!)... Each day wherever possible, make a space in your diary for a buffer zone so you still have another block of time to have another crack at finishing something.  AND if you have finished everything, then you can relax and spend that time on YOU! *Wooooo hoooo!*

Remember what we focus on is forever changing so you need to be flexible and be prepared to allow for changes to your lifestyle (like babies, retirement).  Under-commit rather than over-commit every chance you get so you can stop and smell the roses.  We've all got 24 hours in the day, so make the most of yours every moment you get!

# Home Health Tips

**A house is built with bricks and stone**
**A home is built with love alone**

## For the Body

Did you know there are a *STACK* of fantastic 'natural' alternatives to assisting your body to look, feel and heal well? Essential oils are fantastic to help treat all sorts of ailments from colds and flus to tummy aches and skin conditions and are the perfect remedy for emotional conditions like stress, anxiety and depression. Here are some hints and tips we found interesting ...

**Face Steam:** Fill a bowl with very hot water and add 3-4 drops of some cleansing oils (cypress, eucalyptus, lavender, rosemary). Place a towel over the head and allow the steam to cause the skin to sweat. Your nose may start to run - let it! Steaming is very cleansing and refreshing not to mention good for the head too!

**Puffy Eyes:** Place cold Chamomile tea bags over the eye area, lie down and relax for 10 minutes.

**Cleanser:** Use a small amount of jojoba oil, gently rub onto the face and remove with cotton pads followed by a nice warm compress.

**Toner:** Add 1 drop each of orange, lavender, eucalyptus and geranium into a 100ml spritzer bottle filled with pure water. Shake vigorously and spray onto clean face.

**Face Mask:** Whisk an egg white using a fork then add a little lemon juice. Spread over a cleaned face. Let mixture dry on skin for 10 minutes, remove with warm, wet washer.

**Exfoliant:** Sea salt is a very effective exfoliant. Wet the entire body and rub with salt blended with a couple of drops of your favourite oil. Your skin will really come alive!

**Cucumber Hair Drench:** Blend 1 egg, 2 tbs. olive oil and ¼ of a peeled cucumber until smooth. Spread evenly through your hair, leave on for 10 minutes, then thoroughly rinse. For the best results year round, continue this treatment monthly.

*For more information relating to this see www.readmylips.com*

# For the House

Similarly, there are many effective products probably already in your *PANTRY* that will clean your home just as well but without the chemicals and the expense of the bought products. Here are a few of our favourites ...

**Bicarbonate of soda:** Is a deodoriser which neutralizes odours. Use it powdered or mixed with water. Place baking soda in an open container of your choice. Good for closets, refrigerators and other small enclosed spaces. Use it on your body or in the laundry. Sprinkle on a damp cloth as a non-abrasive cleanser.

**Lemon juice:** Is a mild bleach, a deodorant, a cleaning and polishing agent that will soften stains and repel insects. Roll the lemon before you cut it to maximise the juice.

**White vinegar:** Kills bacteria and can neutralise grease and soap residue. Fill a spray bottle with straight white vinegar to replace your current spray cleaner. Tip: Use cider vinegar to promote blood circulation and regulate the Ph of the skin. It is also an excellent water softener and in a cup or bowl rids rooms of odours.

**Essential oils:** Eucalyptus oil will remove grease, gum and stubborn stains on clothes, it will also help alleviate colds and congestion by rubbing into the base of your foot before bed. Use tea tree or lavender for anti-bacterial and healing uses on the body or in cleaning. Use lavender oil as an effective insect repellent.

**Borax:** Is a naturally occurring mineral salt. It cleans, deodorises, bleaches and disinfects and is useful in the laundry as a soap booster. Borax is also used to control pests such as ants and cockroaches.

**Methylated spirits:** Kills bacteria, whilst shining and polishing porcelain and glass surfaces. You cannot go past 'metho' for cleaning the hand basin, tiles and surface of your bath, and because of its sterilising abilities it is great for the toilet seat. Use it from a spray bottle with a microfibre cloth to buff surfaces to a shine. Spray it on glass and wipe off with old newspaper for gleaming windows and mirrors. Use 1 part 'metho' to 2 parts water to clean polished floor boards, they will come up sparkling every time.

# Handy Home Tips

### More useful tips for cleaning, cooking, laundry and general remedies for the household.

---

**Avoid freezing soups with:** Seafood, potatoes or pasta in them as the texture of these ingredients will suffer.

**Balloons:** Party balloons are easier to blow up if they're submerged in hot water for a few seconds beforehand.

**Body scrub:** Mix together 1 cup sea salt, ½ tsp. ground ginger, ½ tsp. ground cinnamon, 1 cup almond oil. Dampen face with water, then gently rub scrub all over. Wait 5 minutes before rinsing with warm water.

**Caster sugar:** If you run out, ordinary sugar can be ground fine enough in a blender or food processor to substitute.

**Children's doonas:** Place doonas into king-sized covers and tuck the overlap under the mattress to prevent the doonas slipping off.

**Chrome showerheads:** To clean chrome showerheads, fill a plastic bag with vinegar, fit it over the showerhead with an elastic band, leave for a few hours, brush out holes and rinse.

**Citrus tip:** To get more juice from citrus fruit, microwave them for 10 seconds before juicing ... *You'll be amazed!!!*

**Coffee:** As an alternative to sugar sweetening your coffee, try adding a few drops of vanilla.

**Cold sores:** Dab a little bit of acidophilus yoghurt on sore 3 times a day and watch it disappear! Also drinking Yakult will help it go quickly too.

---

**Cooking sprays:** For a cheaper alternative, fill a plastic spray bottle with cooking oil, and use to grease cake tins and baking trays.

**Crumbed food:** For tasty crumbed food, use seasoned stuffing mix instead of the usual breadcrumbs ... Fabulous!

**Crummy tip:** Save all biscuit crumbs in a jar, sweet, savoury and all. When you have enough add butter to make the base of a cheese-cake.

**Deodorise drains:** To deodorise and unclog drains, pour in ½ cup bicarb. of soda followed by 1 cup of white vinegar and allow to sit. Flush with hot water then cold.

**Dirty or greasy fingerprints:** To remove from painted walls, try rubbing the area with a slice of white bread – it works wonders!

**Dog wash:** For an inexpensive shampoo, use a few drops of eucalyptus wool wash. It will give your pet a really shiny coat and keep fleas away. Always apply to the neck area first, this prevents fleas running into your pet's ears for safety.

**Dried out felt tip pens:** Dip tip in white vinegar for five seconds.

**Dry rumble:** To reduce the time that your wet towels need to be tumble dried, add an already dry towel to the wet load. It really works!

**Eggs:** To check if an egg is fresh, pop it in a glass of water. A stale egg will float vertically; a fresh egg will lie horizontally on the bottom of the glass.

**Fragrant feet:** Put a pinch of bicarb. of soda in your shoes each day before you wear them. It's simple, cheap and very effective.

**Frayed ribbons:** Paint the end of a ribbon with clear nail polish.

**Fried eggs:** When frying eggs, chop an onion and use the large outer rings as egg rings. This tastes great and saves you washing sticky egg off metal rings.

**Flat softdrinks:** Rather than throwing them out, freeze and turn into icy poles. Kids love them and they are cheap!

 **Flushing the toilet:** To cut back the use of water in older toilets, remove labels from a 1 litre plastic bottle and fill with water and place in the cistern.

**Fruit salad:** Improve flavour of fruit salads by adding ½ cup lemonade; this will also help keep it fresh for several days.

**Get rid of ants:** Put small piles of cornmeal where you see ants. They eat it, take it 'home,' can't digest it so it kills them. Similarly, dog flea powder. Sprinkle a little on an ant nest and it'll send them scurrying!

**Goodbye fruit flies:** To get rid of pesky fruit flies, take a small glass, fill it half way with apple cider vinegar and 2 drops of dish washing liquid. Mix well. You will find those flies drawn to the cup and gone forever!

**Great crumbs:** To make your own breadcrumbs, grate frozen bread – this is far easier than trying to grate fresh bread.

**Hair conditioner:** Use your hair conditioner to shave your legs. It's a lot cheaper than shaving cream and leaves your legs really smooth. It's also a great way to use up the conditioner you bought but didn't like when you tried it in your hair.

**Homemade cakes and biscuits:** Stay fresh longer by placing a sugar cube in the container when storing them.

**If you feel a cold coming on:** Rub some eucalyptus on the soles of your feet before you go to bed and you'll find that the symptoms will soon dissipate.

**Ironing jeans:** Place them in the freezer first for 30 minutes. You'll find the iron glides over the material and creases iron out easier. Same principle for candle wax off candle holders.

**Laundry detergents:** Use a phosphate-free laundry detergent when washing as this will be much safer to use on gardens and pot plants.

**Leaves:** Rake autumn leaves into heaps, then hose lightly. Damp leaves are easier to handle and you can fit more into a bag or bin.

**Lemon saver:** When a recipe calls for a squeeze of lemon juice, pierce a lemon with a knitting needle and use the required amount. The lemon can then be stored in fridge and reused.

**Measuring cups:** Before you pour sticky substances into a measuring cup, fill with hot water. Dump out the hot water, but don't dry cup. Next, add your ingredient, such as peanut butter, and watch how easily it comes out.

**New shoes:** If your new shoes are blistering your heel, rub a plain candle against the section of the shoe causing the problem.

**No more mosquitoes:** Place a dryer sheet in your pocket. It will keep the mosquitoes away.

**Opened softdrinks:** If you have no cap to reseal an open softdrink, an uninflated balloon fitted over the neck of the bottle works a treat.

**Out of chutney:** Combine ½ cup plum jam, with ¼ cup sultanas add a splash of Worcestershire sauce to taste ... *It's just as good!*

**Piece of cake:** When testing to see if your cake is baked right thorough, push a length of raw spaghetti into the centre of the cake. If spaghetti comes out clean and dry, the cake is done.

**Plastic containers:** To prevent containers from being stained by tomato based sauces, spray with non-stick cooking spray beforehand.

**Plum pudding:** When boiling a plum pudding in a cloth, add slices of lemon to the boiling water to prevent the cloth sticking to the pudding.

**Reducing static cling:** Pin a small safety pin to the seam of your garment and you will not have a clingy skirt or dress. Same thing works with pants that cling when wearing stockings. Place pin in the seam and ta da! Static is gone.

**Reopening envelope:** If you seal an envelope and then realize you forgot to include something inside, just place your sealed envelope in the freezer for an hour or two. It unseals easily.

**Roast chicken:** Rub mayonnaise into the skin of the chicken before cooking. It results in a lovely crisp skin.

**Rusted bolts:** To loosen a rusted bolt, apply a cloth soaked in Coke to the rust and hold it in place for several minutes!

**Soup not flavoursome enough:** Add seasonings such as cloves, peppercorns and bay leaves.

**To remove a splinter:** From a small child, put a little teething gel around it to numb and soften the skin.

**Shabby flowers:** Remove from vase, plunge into bucket of boiling water and allow to cool. Remove, cut stems on an angle and place back into vase with fresh water.

**Stainless steel:** To keep your trendy stainless steel kitchen appliances shiny and smudge free, spray some WD40 onto a soft cloth and wipe over surfaces for a gleaming finish.

**Stains on white fabric:** Simply apply a thick layer of toothpaste. Leave overnight before rinsing off.

**Stuffed toys:** To rid toys and teddies of stale smells, place in a paper bag with some baking soda. Shake the bag for a minute, remove toy, brush off remaining powder and pop them in the sun for a while.

**Substitute oil in a stir fry:** Heat a spoonful of sesame seeds in the pan, they produce their own oil and add a wonderful flavour to the dish.

**Sweet sauce:** Save the juice from canned fruits and thicken with cornflour or custard powder for a tasty, sweet sauce to serve with puddings and cakes. Or pour it into ice-block moulds and freeze. Add fresh fruit for a healthy summer treat for the kids.

**To shave chocolate:** Refrigerate until cold, then use a potato peeler.

**To stop your avocado dip from going brown:** Place the avocado seed under the dip mixture. It will stay greener much longer.

**Toilet cleaner and bathroom soap scum cleaner:** Mix 2 parts bleach and 1 part water in a spray bottle and every fortnight spray the glass and tiles in the shower, bathroom basins and also the toilet bowl to keep each looking like brand new and sparkling clean.

**Tulips:** To prevent drooping, add a few drops of vodka to the water.

**Weeds:** For an environmentally friendly weed killer simply use white vinegar. Just spray it directly onto weeds. Or try boiling hot water too.

# Budget Menu Ideas

There are plenty of recipes from within the pages of 4 Ingredients 2 that will help you impress any gathering on any occasion.

Here are a couple of examples, that people just like you suggested!!!

## Date Night Menu

**You must be the change you wish to see in the world.**
**Mahatma Ghandi**

---

**NIBBLE**

*Feta Dip  p. 21*
*Served with:  Melba toast*
*&*
*fresh, julienned vegetables*

**ENTRE**

*Tomato Soup   p. 68*
*Served with:  Fresh crusty bread*

**MAIN**

*Veal & Pesto Rolls   p. 110*
*Served with:  Mashed Potato   p. 88*
*&*
*Herbed Zucchini   p. 95*

**DESSERT**

*Baked Apples with a Twist   p. 160*

# Girls Luncheon Menu

"My boyfriend used to ask his mother, 'How can I find the right woman for me?' and she would answer, 'Don't worry about finding the right woman, concentrate on becoming the right man.'"

**Unknown**

---

### NIBBLES

*Asparagus Wraps  p. 37*
*&*
*Baked Haloumi  p. 37*

### LUNCH

*Balsamic Glazed Lamb Cutlets  p. 129*
*Served with:  Feta & Watermelon Salad  p. 80*

### DESSERT

*Toblerone Dip  p. 24*
*Served with:  A mezze of fresh, sliced fruit*

### DRINKS

*Mint Tea  p. 178*
*or*
*A glass of Bubbles*

# Vegetarian Dinner Party Menu

*"Nothing will benefit human health and increase the chances for survival of life on Earth as much as the evolution to a vegetarian diet."*

**Albert Einstein**

---

### NIBBLES

*Warm Cheese Dip  p. 25*
*Served with:  Slices of fresh, crusty bread*
*&*
*a mezze of fresh vegetables*

### ENTRE

*Tempting Mini-Pizzas  p. 46*

### MAIN

*Baked Ricotta Pie  p. 150*
*Served with:   Green salad drizzled with a*
*delicious Balsamic Dressing  p. 26*

### DESSERT

*Frozen Yoghurt Tarts p. 166*

# A Bachelor's Guide to Dinner

*A computer once beat me at chess,*
*but it was no match for me at kick boxing !!!!!*

**Emo Philips**

---

**NIBBLES**

*Easy Pork Bites p. 143*

**MAIN**

*BBQ Beef Stir Fry p. 100*
*Served with: Boiled Rice*

**DESSERT**

*Little Lemon Cheesecakes p. 167*

# Kid's Party Ideas

We worry about what a child will become tomorrow,
yet we forget that he is someone today.

### Stacia Tauscher

---

### NIBBLES

*Fruit Kebabs*
*Date Slice  p. 196*
*Pikelets  p. 58*

### LUNCH

*Chicken Carnival Cones  p. 183*
*Sausage Rolls  p. 77*
*Mini-Cheese Quiches  p. 187*

### DESSERT

*Caramel, Choc Truffles  p. 193*
*Jelly in Oranges  p. 198*
*Birthday Cake*

### DRINKS

*Water*

*Served with:  Ice-cubes that have been frozen with a drop of
food colouring in them. You can make different colours for a
pretty rainbow effect!*

---

# Biographies

## Kim McCosker

Kim was born in Stanthorpe but raised in Mundubbera, Queensland, a fantastic little town where her wonderful family and many of her beautiful friends still live. Schooled on the Gold Coast, Kim attended Star of the Sea Catholic High School and Griffith University, completing a Bachelor of International Finance. Kim trained with MLC as a Financial Planner, completing her Diploma in Financial Planning through Deakin University in 2000. Kim's natural ease with people, her ability to communicate effortlessly and her country confidence served her extremely well as a successful financial adviser and later as the Queensland State Manager of MLC Private Client Services. After the birth of her second child, Kim resigned and decided to contract from home writing financial plans.

It was during this phase of her life that 4 Ingredients was brought into a reality. Kim had the idea, but it was at the insistence of her life-long friend Rachael Bermingham that they write the book ... And so over a couple of red wines began the wonderful rollercoaster ride 4 Ingredients would go on to become!

Taking a year to compile and cook, 4 Ingredients (or Kim's fourth child as she lovingly refers to it) was launched on the 14th March 2007. From an initial print run of 2,000 that was deemed "over-ambitious in a market saturated with cookbooks" Kim and Rachael went on to orchestrate what the book trade refers to as "an absolute phenomenon" ie., a book that ended 2007 as one of the biggest selling books, across all genres, in both Australia and New Zealand.

And as Kim says "No-one was more surprised than us!"

In addition to this, over the past 8 years, Glen and Kim have bought and renovated several properties, including a 1957 Anglican Church, a beachside shack, and the current house they now live in on the

Sunshine Coast's beautiful Pelican Waters.  They own 'relic', an antique, retro store in Brisbane's trendy West End and co-own a fabulous café in Mundubbera called 'Bella Boo.'  Kim maintains the administration, bookwork and finances for their various businesses and financial interests.

Without a sliver of doubt however, the most rewarding of everything accomplished to date has been the birth of her three precious little boys Morgan 6, Hamilton 3 and Flynn, 2 months old.  For Kim, family is THE MOST IMPORTANT and carries the greatest priority of all she does!  Renovations to properties were done with the children playing in the yard, recipes tested with them mixing and stirring, books written around their sleeptimes and trips made only when her wonderfully supportive and very loved husband Glen could be home for them.

Life presents many opportunities, but having the courage to pursue them, in what is an ever increasingly busy and demanding world, is hard.  But Kim is living proof that you can achieve whatever you want in life with exactly that ... *Hard work!*

You can contact Kim through:
>        the 4 Ingredients website **www.4Ingredients.com.au** or
>        by emailing her at **kim@4ingredients.com.au**

# Rachael Bermingham

Rachael Bermingham (nee Moore) was born in Stanthorpe before moving to the Sunshine Coast at 11 where she grew up & still resides with husband Paul (a renovator) & gorgeous son Jaxson 3. She is also 'wicked' step mum to Lee 19 & Teri 17.

Working from her home office, Rachael co-runs 4 Ingredients & Sunshine Coast Speakers & solo operates her personal speaking engagements & Read My Lips: her 1st self published book she co-wrote to inspire women to achieve their goals (first published 14/2/06) which she penned out while feeding baby Jaxson.

A born entrepreneur Rachael showed her keen eye for business early on with the launch of her first business venture (the first mobile hair salon on the Sunshine Coast) at age 19 that she built up for a year, & sold for a profit before going onto experience a host of bold careers to satisfy her adventurous nature, including diving & shark feeding at Underwater World before her passion for business returned in the form of travel.

After a 5 year stint as a Flight Centre travel agent, Rachael entered into what could have been considered a fatal business move by opening her own travel agency just 3 months prior to September 11. This experience would ultimately prove to be a pivotal point in her career igniting the development of an ability which would be invaluable for Rachael, Read My Lips & 4 Ingredients & inspire others in business around the world as well.

With the travel trade in a spin, Rachael didn't give up; instead she worked well into the early morning hours teaching herself how to market so her business would survive in the industry's most ruinous era. Researching & testing LOTS & LOTS (& LOTS!) of strategies, she learnt the art of marketing & found she LOVED it & thankfully had a real knack for it.

Her talent for marketing & publicity soon became well known and requests from others to help them also started coming in. She sat on various business boards including an RSL, town developmental board and a business women's board before leaving travel to take on the first of many businesses she would build from a tiny turnover to an astonishing MULTI MILLION dollar turnovers within months AND without spending a cent on advertising! Right up to an hour of going into labour, Rachael was still actively involved in mentoring and helping business owners in 6 different countries.

Within days of becoming a Mum, Rachael known for her abundant energy & enthusiasm continued to pursue her passion for business instigating a motivational seminar for women encompassing life, health, wealth and business success strategies with the help of some of girlfriends that ran for 2 years and morphed into the book Read My Lips.

It was by giving Read My Lips to Kim as a gift at Jaxsons 1st birthday party that would prove to be the beginning of yet another incredible journey for Rachael. Prompted by Rachael's passing comment of 'They say everyone has a good book in them' Kim entrusted her own fabulous idea for a book with Rachael (a cookbook using a few ingredients) which Rachael immediately loved and proceeded to prod Kim to start compiling (mainly so Rachael herself could use it!!!) Kim after a few weeks said that she'd do it on the condition 'that you write it with me!'. And the rest is beautiful history!

These days when Rachael's not enjoying time with her family, cooking up a storm with Kim, or working on other books, she loves speaking at conferences to inspire others to achieve their own goals. She also enjoys talking on time management, life balance, how to develop a business from home and of course marketing and publicity.

You can contact Rachael by email;
   **rachael@4ingredients.com.au**
   Or by snail mail; **PO Box 1171 Mooloolaba QLD 4557**

Rachael's other business website links;
   Read My Lips **www.ReadMyLips.com**

Speaking Information and bookings
   **www.RachaelBermingham.com**

Sunshine Coast Speakers
   **www.SunshineCoastSpeakers.com**

# Bibliography

## Books

Cyndi O'Meara. **Changing Habits Changing Lives.**
Penguin Books Victoria, Australia 2000.

Cyndi O'Meara. **Changing Habits Changing Lives Cookbook.**
Penguin Books Victoria, Australia 2002.

Kim Morrison and Fleur Welligan. **Like Chocolate for Women**.
Random House. Auckland, New Zealand 2004.

Kim Morrison and Fleur Welligan. **About Face**.
Random House. Auckland, New Zealand 2007.

Nestle. **Sweet Treats – 50 Family Favourites.**
FPC Living (Books Division) General Newspapers Pty Ltd, 2002.

Culinary Arts Institute. **Encyclopaedic Cookbook**.
Book Production Industries, Inc. Chicago, Illinois, 1959.

Bay Books. **Mother's Favourite Recipes – the Best of Traditional Home Cooking**. Bay Books 61-69 Anzac Parade, Kensington NSW 2033, 1985.

Margaret Fulton. **Encyclopaedia of Food & Cookery**.
Octopus Pty Ltd. 44 Market Street, Sydney, NSW 2000, 1983.

**The Presbyterian Cookery Book**. Compiled for The Women's Missionary Association of the Presbyterian Church of New South Wales. 1950.

Anne Marshall. **Anne's Perfect Piebook.** Paul Hamlyn Pty Ltd. 176 South Creek Road, Dee Why West New South Wales 2099. 1979.

**Small Food**. Murdoch Books. GPO Box 1203 Sydney, New South Wales 1045. 2002.

A Parragon Book. **Perfect Tapas.**
Parragon 4 Queens Street Bath BA1 1HE, UK. 2007.

Anne Thorpe. **The Australian Cookbook.**
Child & Henry Publishing P/L 9 Clearview Place, Brookvale, NSW 2100.

Gabrielle Bluett. **50 Easy Low Salt Recipes.** Self-published. 8/46 Muston Street, Mosman NSW 2088.

# Webpages

Winter Fruits – April – December
//www.aumann.com.au/fruit-winter.htm


Baby Food:
//www.essentialbaby.com.au/page/essential_recipes.html

//www.wholesomebabyfood.com/baby-food-freezing-chart.htm


"Leftover Rescue Tips" December 2003
//www.recipezaar.com


"What to do with leftover chicken dishes"
//www.leftoverchicken.com/recipes/view_recipe.php?recipeid=26


"Remains of the day: why eating leftovers can save the planet."

//blogs.smh.com.au/lifestyle/chewonthis/archives/2007/11/remains_of_
the_day_eat_leftove.html


"Footprints: Tread lightly into the future.
//www.northsydney.nsw.gov.au/footprints/resources_cleaning.asp


Poems for Parents
//home.att.net/~DLeddy/ppoems.html


Laurent Caters for Kids
//www.laurentcaters.com.au


//www.readmylips.com

# Notes

# Notes

# Notes

# Notes

# Index of Contents

## Light Meals & Lunches — 64

### Soups — 64

### All Others — 69

## Sides — 80

## Salads — 80

## Potato — 86

## Vegetables — 92

# Invitation

To all who contributed a recipe to this book by way of email, post or phone we would like to extend a *sincere* thank you.

If *YOU* have a fabulous 4 or 5 ingredient recipe and think that others would enjoy cooking it please submit it at: www.4ingredients.com.au be sure to include name, suburb or town for acknowledgment.

# *Thank You*

Best Wishes & Happy Cooking

# KIM& RACHAEL

Kim          Rachael

www.4ingredients.com.au

4

*Ingredients*
2